James Sta

Susan Allen Toth

A HOUSE OF ONE'S OWN

A HOUSE OF ONE'S OWN

AN ARCHITECT'S GUIDE TO DESIGNING THE HOUSE OF YOUR DREAMS

JAMES STAGEBERG   SUSAN ALLEN TOTH

Clarkson Potter/Publishers
New York

For Edgar Clarence Stageberg of Dawson, Minnesota
(1892–1947)

We are grateful for a quarter's leave granted to James for work on this book by Harrison Fraker, Dean of the College of Architecture at the University of Minnesota.

We also wish to thank Dennis Sachs and Bill Beyer, partners in The Stageberg Partners, for their support and encouragement; Jim Foran, whose invaluable help we mention in the following pages; Vickie Abrahamson, whose ideas sparked our own; Leonard Parker, who assured us we could indeed do this; Molly Friedrich, our agent, quick of mind and strong of heart; and Lauren Shakely, our careful and clear-sighted editor, who cheered us on.

We are also thankful to James's clients, past and present, who have provided him with opportunities for house design.

For any errors and omissions, we alone are responsible.

"Cabin Fever: The Client's Final Report" originally appeared in a slightly different form in *MPLS/St. Paul* magazine

AIA Document B141, Standard Form of Agreement Between Owner and Architect, 13th Edition (page 183), copyright ©1977, reprinted by permission of the American Institute of Architects

Published by Clarkson Potter/Publishers, 201 East 50th Street, New York, New York 10022. Member of the Crown Publishing Group.

CLARKSON POTTER, POTTER and colophon are trademarks of Clarkson N. Potter, Inc.

Manufactured in the United States of America

Book design by Renato Stanisic

Photographs by Christian Korab
and Lea Babcock

Illustrations by James Stageberg, Jim Foran, and Tom Jenkinson

Library of Congress Cataloging-in-Publication Data

Stageberg, James.
    A house of one's own: an architect's guide to designing the house of your dreams / James Stageberg and Susan Allen Toth.
        p.   cm.
      1. Architect-designed houses.   2. Architects and patrons.
    I. Toth, Susan Allen.   II. Title.
    NA7115.S7   1991
    728'.37—dc20   90-22366

ISBN 0-517-58214-7

10 9 8 7 6 5 4 3 2 1

First Edition

CONTENTS

AUTHORS' NOTE

One of us is an architect, and the other is a writer. When we decided to collaborate, we knew that we each had skills the other could only dabble in. What brought us together on this book was a shared love of houses—James's a lifetime and professional commitment, Susan's an amateur's fascination—and our delight in planning, building and decorating our Wisconsin retreat, Wind Whistle. It seemed natural to combine James's years of training and practice in house design with Susan's prose.

Since we each respected the other's expertise, we worked on the text together fairly easily. First we discussed the general topics we wanted to cover, and Susan raised some specific questions she felt a client might like answered. James made notes and then wrote out a rough draft of his ideas. Susan rewrote the draft, edited, and asked more questions—which usually meant, for James, more notes and more rough drafts, as well as sessions at the computer when James talked and Susan typed. Both of us scrutinized the final text, and we feel jointly responsible for it.

We owe a special debt to Jim Foran, an architect with The Stageberg

Partners and our longtime friend. He served as James's architectural sounding board, the kind of good and honest critic every designer needs. He helped at every stage of the house, valiantly wading through poison ivy to assess the site and assisting with the various drawings that accompany the text.

One editorial note may clear up some pronoun confusion. Although women are still, regrettably, a minority of architects, more and more are entering the profession. Although the double pronoun ("he or she") is awkward, we have used it rather than the indefinite "he." Even in small grammatical matters, anything we can do to counteract the impression that architects are always men may be useful.

Although we wrote the text together, James is speaking as the "I" throughout, since these are *his* ideas and experiences as an architect. The exceptions are here, in our "Authors' Note," and in chapters 14 and 16, when Susan is writing from *her* ideas and experiences.

The first part of our book talks about the general process of house design. In the second part we discuss how these general principles applied to the design and construction of Wind Whistle.

Work, love, build a house, and die. But build a house.
                    —*Donald Hall,* The One Day

WORKING WITH AN ARCHITECT

PART ONE

THE ARCHITECT'S INTRODUCTION

This short book is not meant to replace architects. After designing many houses over the past thirty years, I believe that a designer needs both study and experience to create a satisfying, workable house. For something more than workable—for something wonderful—a designer also needs talent and inspiration. If a would-be architect could simply read these notes of mine and design a wonderful house immediately, I would be a member of a vanishing profession.

I hope general readers who are interested in the design and construction of houses will enjoy this book. Three more specific groups of readers may also find it valuable: those who are curious about what an architect does; those who want to hire an architect to design a house and need to know how to contribute to the process; and those who plan to design their own houses.

The third category, home builders who feel they can get along just fine without architects, is an audience my profession likes to ignore. After all, they do not give us any commissions. Naturally, I wish they

3

would. It would be marvelous if everyone wanted and could afford an architect. I'd like to live in a world in which design was so important that every family could live in a beautiful house, no matter how modest.

Of course, not every beautiful house needs an architect. Some cultures have an indigenous architecture that is harmonious and pleasing, a common art form that has developed over centuries. Several years ago, when Susan and I honeymooned on the remote Sicilian island of Pantelleria, I was struck by the simple elegance of the generic house, the dome-shaped stone *dammuso*. It used local materials (Pantelleria is essentially treeless), protected the inhabitants from the fierce Mediterranean sun, and provided an economical living space. The graceful curving shapes, multiplied hundreds of times on a rocky hillside, blended into the landscape like sculpture, and when whitewashed, gleamed in the sun with dazzling brightness. Though limited in spatial terms, the design of the *dammuso* gives pleasure to the eye and spirit.

When I travel around America, I seldom see domestic architecture that combines economy with beauty. We are a nation of fierce individualists, and almost everyone wants a house that is a little different —only not *too* different! Some people are undoubtedly afraid of having an architect tell them what to do and what kind of house to have. They want to do it themselves. The result is often a hodgepodge of forms, sprawling boxes, jarring angles, Cyclops-eyed gables, anachronistic or clichéd ornament, and tedious landscaping.

Most people are unaware not only of how to create an aesthetic whole, but of the small but crucial decisions that make a plan work. In one new house I recently visited, when I asked to use the bathroom, my hostess seemed a little embarrassed as she directed me to the door, which opened almost directly into the living room. She immediately began a loud conversation with my wife, and I turned the faucets on full.

While this book will not turn every home builder into a designer, I hope it will help those who are planning their dream houses to avoid such mistakes. Just as important, I hope it will stimulate do-it-yourselfers to think through some larger questions—about the nature of their site, for example, or how they feel about light—before they begin to build.

For those who have decided to find an architect to design a custom-built home, this book should be a useful tool in all stages of the process, from choosing the right architect to compiling the final "punch list." (In Chapter 10, "When Is Your House Really Finished?" we explain what a punch list is.) Show your architect this book (lend him or her your copy, or, even better, as Susan the writer always says, tell the architect to *buy* a copy). He or she may want to comment on, disagree with, or add to the observations in the book, which is fine. The more informed discussion you can have with an architect, the better you will feel about working together.

For anyone who is curious about how architects actually work, this book should give some prolonged glimpses over an architect's shoulder onto scraps of paper, sketches, working drawings, and some of the notes that accumulate on the drafting table. I have tried to show how a practicing architect thinks in both aesthetic and functional terms—the two have to be constantly joined in one's mind—and how those thoughts get transferred first into two and then into three dimensions. In Part Two, "At Work on Wind Whistle," I discuss the process of creating one particular house, again trying to show how an architect creates, adapts, changes, and works on a design.

We did not plan this book to appeal to architectural historians or theorists. Although I can find architectural theory fascinating (when I understand it), I have always been a "hands-on" kind of architect. I design houses with sketches, and until I began to put down in words what I've learned from my years of practice, I didn't realize what strong ideas I had about so many subjects!

For a recent book that does describe how one architect approached his own house design in a variety of cultural and personal contexts, I recommend Witold Rybczynski's *The Most Beautiful House in the World*.

When I first paged through Rybczynski's book, I was puzzled, because I was eager to see pictures of "the most beautiful house in the world" and didn't find any. I finally realized, as he explained on page 186, that he believes "the most beautiful house in the world is the one you build for yourself." I respect his aesthetic criterion, but I don't happen to agree with it, probably because, years ago, when I was a very young architect, I did indeed not only design but actually build a house for myself. It was definitely *not* the most beautiful house in the world. After a while, although I continued to respect it, I didn't even like it.

This book will not tell you step by step how to construct a house. For such a meticulous, detailed account of building practices, consult Jim Locke's *The Well-Built House,* which is a welcome companion to Tracy Kidder's *House,* a fascinating day-to-day account of how one particular house was built. Locke offers much technical information, undoubtedly useful to those who are planning to build or remodel houses themselves. He doesn't seem to like architects very much, and he recommends that you choose a builder first and let the builder select the designer. As you will be able to tell from the following pages, I take an exactly opposite approach. I *do* like and respect builders, at least all the ones who have worked with me on my houses, but I believe that construction should follow design, which the architect provides.

Susan and I hope our book will make your own involvement with house design, and with architects, more meaningful and useful.

HOW TO SELECT
AN ARCHITECT

Every architect would probably give a potential client slightly different guidelines on how to select the right designer for his or her house. One standard tactic is to call the local chapter of our professional organization, the American Institute of Architects, for a list of names. Following this method, however, the client will get a rather bland list. Someone in the office will simply say, "These people do houses," without any particular recommendation. As a matter of policy, professional organizations can hardly play favorites or go on record about the personality or peculiarities of any particular architect.

It is hard for me to imagine hiring an architect without considering his or her personality. An architect has to create something from nothing, and to do that, he or she needs to have a distinctive style. I don't think I've ever known a significant architect, or even a promising architectural student, who didn't have a strong personality. I didn't always like that personality, but it was certainly there. On the other hand, a blah person will probably produce a blah house.

That personality had better strike a responsive chord with the client. Not only will you be working together on the house, sharing intimate detail about your daily life and routines, but you will want a final result that is compatible with your own personal style.

So another approach to hiring an architect is more roundabout but ultimately more fulfilling. You might begin by inquiring about who designed a house that provokes your admiration or at least your curiosity. Perhaps a friend will suggest an architect whom another friend has liked. Ask an architect to suggest some architects. (Obviously, you'll need to use some tact with this approach; don't ask for suggestions from an architect who designs houses if you don't plan to include him or her on your list!)

Once you have a list of recommendations, call each of the architects on your list, explain that you are considering building a house, and ask for an appointment to visit the office and see some of the firm's work, probably initially from photographs and models. Don't feel that you need to offer the job to the first one who spends some time with you, or indeed to any of them. Architects expect to be interviewed. They also learn to expect some of their potential clients to go out the door and find another architect.

Use this interview not only to learn some of the basic facts about how the architect works but also to get a sense of the architect's personality. Trust your intuition. If the architect greets you in a flowing cape and dramatic hat, reminiscent of Frank Lloyd Wright, and you have been buying the same gray suit at Brooks Brothers for twenty years, you might ask yourself whether you are really ready for some drama in your house.

If an architect explains his or her work with incomprehensible jargon, don't necessarily feel either that you are very dumb or that the architect is very smart. In a world that more and more prizes professional mumbo-jumbo as a sign of intellectual and social prestige, architects sometimes try to grab their share by speaking in their own special and impenetrable language. If, soon after you've sat down to talk, the architect begins to tell you the "intellectual raison d'être" behind his or her practice, listen carefully. If what you hear doesn't make sense, beware. You're going to need to be able to communicate clearly with your future architect at all stages of the design process. If he or she says, "What matters here is the viability of the spatial concept, related to the environmental aesthetic in three-dimensional terms, though not in a deconstructivist sense," you should decide if you enjoy such conversation. If you go with this architect you're probably going to hear a lot of it.

Of course, if you know something about architectural training and historical styles, you can ask your architect whether he or she is part of a particular tradition or movement. Probe his or her opinions about broken pediments, postmodernism, or the Bauhaus. Chat about Prairie Style homes, California ramblers, and Dutch colonials. But pay more attention to the finished work the architect shows you. Buildings speak louder than words, and you are hiring a skilled designer/practitioner, not a philosopher or an architectural debater.

At some point in your conversation, one of you will have to raise the issue of how much the house will cost. If the architect seems uncomfortable talking about money or sounds unnecessarily vague about costs, you had better think about shopping elsewhere. You are going to have to make many decisions in conjunction with your architect about budgets and expenditures, from whether to build your garage now or later to what kind of faucets you want in the bathroom. You can't be hemming and hawing every time the subject of money comes up.

What does an architect cost, and how does he or she charge for services? Like a lawyer, an architect bases a fee on the number of hours the job will require from his or her office and professional staff. Many of the best architects will only commit themselves to a job that will be "full service," which means the architect will be part of the project from beginning to end. The architect not only will program, design, develop construction drawings, and select a builder, but will keep an alert eye on the process of construction and consult with the owners about potential or real problems after they have moved into the house.

At the lower end of the scale of service (or lack of it), I know that on the bulletin board at our architectural school, I often see notices from prospective clients wanting to hire a student to draw up plans for their house. (I somehow doubt you'd find similar notices on the bulletin boards at our medical or law schools from someone who wanted a third-year student to take out an appendix or litigate a divorce.)

In between these extremes, an architect may agree to perform partial services, such as design-only, or interpreting a plan from a magazine into more personal terms, or working on a house until the actual digging begins. In my experience, most of the horror stories new homeowners tell about architects are a result of hiring an architect for less than full service. The architect has not necessarily acted incompetently, but "partial service" does not require—or engage—an architect's full attention to every detail. The corners, edges, and sometimes even the critical middle may not be covered.

Every architect is open to negotiating his or her fee, although of course an extremely popular or busy architect may only do so under special circumstances. I usually charge 10 percent of construction costs for new houses and up to 15 percent for additions or remodeling, fees that may be slightly higher than those of some of my local colleagues, but certainly less than those of famous architects like Philip Johnson or I. M. Pei. Charging a percentage fee, rather than an hourly rate, eliminates a client's worrying about whether redoing a particular part of the plan, for example, will cost more money. (For further discussion of the architect's fee, see Chapter 4, "What Will It All Cost?")

A common and understandable fear about a percentage charge is that it gives a greedy architect an incentive to allow high costs. In fact, much of an architect's job is cutting costs by going "back to the boards" to find a better (and cheaper) way to accomplish a goal, replanning, and restructuring. If an architect acquires a reputation for exceeding estimates, you can be sure he or she won't be recommended by a client to someone else and will not be building houses for very long. (This test of time is another reason to hire a seasoned architect.)

One safeguard that I have found works well for my clients and me is to wait to agree upon the fee until we have the construction estimates. As we talk initially, we both know roughly what the house will have to cost. If my client has $150,000 to spend (not, unfortunately, the extravagant sum it seemed just a few short years ago), I know that I will have to create a design that can be "bid out" for that sum. If the estimate is higher, I'll have to change the design. If it is lower, my client will be very happy. My fee may be slightly less, but the satisfied homeowner will recommend me to someone else.

During the initial interview, besides discussing your expectations about costs, the architect should ask certain critical questions. What are your dreams for your house? What images or pictures do you have in mind? Do you have a site? In the initial interview you will probably not cover the details—whether or not to have a family room, what kind of kitchen cabinets you want, and how many visiting grandchildren you need to plan for. First, you and the architect need to find out if you share the same basic vision of house design.

Later, if you decide to hire this architect, the two of you will spend lots of time talking about detail. (For some information on what in fact will happen next, see Chapter 3, "When an Architect and Client Sit Down to Work.")

While you are interviewing the architect, the architect is probably also interviewing you. No architect wants to work for a client for whom he or she can't do a good job. Maybe *your* personality doesn't seem like the right fit. The architect may subtly or directly discourage you, telling you that the kind of house you have in mind is "not the sort of thing I do." A potential client once came to me for a new house, but his only concern was how expensive and showy it would look from the outside. "My prime requirement," he said, "is that the house be a hundred feet on the street." This was not a client I was anxious to work with.

The architect you're interviewing may not have the courage to tell you he or she doesn't like you, but you'll probably know anyway. If you don't feel wanted, move on. Don't give up on an architect whose work and style you like simply because he or she doesn't fawn over you, however; some architects may not want to give you a hard sell or may be trying to identify exactly what it is you want.

Now you need to look at some of the architect's work, slowly and carefully. Let him or her tell you something about each project, what and who it was planned for, how successfully it turned out, what might have been done differently. Then find out how the architect's designs have lasted over a period of time. Ask to see some examples of work from, say, ten or fifteen years ago. (I'm assuming here that you have gone to an experienced architect who has built many houses; since I think of myself in my sixties as being in my prime, I'm obviously prejudiced in favor of age.) You don't want a house that is modern today, outdated or funny-looking or ugly tomorrow.

You might also look around an architect's office to see if you see any framed awards on the walls. (Most architects display these as proudly and prominently as doctors do their diplomas and certificates of specialization.) Or you can ask, if you have enough nerve, if the architect has any awards you *ought* to see. Listen carefully to the response. The most distinguished design awards are given by an architect's peers, probably the state chapter of the American Institute of Architects, whose "honor awards" are highly coveted. Most prestigious are the national awards of this same organization, also called "honor awards," and given in very limited numbers each year. You should not take too seriously the certificates or prizes given rather freely by builders or trade associations, whose juries are far less concerned with design quality than with successful use of their products—picture windows, for example, or wood siding, or cement blocks.

You might also eye askance awards earned in any category of "innovation." Not long ago I read this blurb in the real estate section of a West Coast newspaper: "Take some architectural touches from yesterday, blend them with spaces designed for the life-styles of today, and add the home technology of tomorrow. The result: NEST (New Expanding Shelter Technology) '89, a modular demonstration home." I wasn't surprised that the writer didn't include a picture of the exterior of this house. A touch of this, a touch of that, and a bit of blending and adding do not usually create a building of any aesthetic distinction.

I'd watch out for signs of determined trendiness in your architect's language and in his or her projects. Although I am fascinated by good new design, especially when it emerges from the individual vision of an outstanding architect, I am wary of what happens to innovation when it is imitated routinely by a less gifted practitioner. Certain words make me wary: "futuristic," "innovative," "style-setting," "eclectic." They sound exciting, but they tend to be like women's fashions. Who wants a house that is dated as fast as one of those bubble dresses?

Classic design can be more genuinely exciting than "innovation," lifting the spirits of the owner with the beauty of its lines and spaces, creating an effect that can be breathtaking rather than bizarre. If the architect you're interviewing insists on how up-to-date he or she is, and implies that "classic" necessarily means "dull," be careful. After all, you plan to live inside this new environment and look at it for at least several years.

As you review the pictures and models the architect shows you, don't assume that any one particular house represents the only style in which an architect can design. When Susan and I show visitors through Wind Whistle, with its bold color and soaring ceilings, I know that many of them are probably thinking, "Not for me! I sure wouldn't want a blue ceiling in *my* bedroom. I'd rather have a big kitchen you can eat in. And who needs a sauna?" (Of course, most of them say very politely, "How nice!")

If they asked, I could tell them that I am used to doing houses in many other formats and designs. I created Wind Whistle for a very particular client, my wife, and it reflects her taste and my own. Just after I finished Wind Whistle, I began work on a house across the Mississippi River from us, a house that is not only much larger but also more formal and more restrained. Instead of brightly painted wood siding, it has an unobtrusive stucco exterior, and all its interior walls —and ceilings!—are white. The owners wanted a quiet house, one that did not draw attention to itself, while Wind Whistle is meant to be exuberant.

Before you conclude your interview with an architect, ask about how he or she handles problems. No house is ever built without some difficulty, and the architect who pretends otherwise doesn't have enough experience or wisdom. So ask him or her to describe for you a few problems that occurred in building a recent house—perhaps one you have just seen in photographs—and then to explain how those problems were resolved.

For example, I could tell a prospective client about a leaky skylight in an addition I designed some years ago for Martin Friedman, the intelligent, astute, and forceful director of the Walker Art Center in Minneapolis. I could vividly describe the pain that owner and architect both felt when water began to drip onto Martin's varnished oak floor. Using Frank Lloyd Wright's often-repeated advice to an owner, "Just put a plant under it," doesn't work. Leaks can be insidious monsters, because you can't always tell where they are coming from, and they show up at the damnedest times, not always consistent with rain, snow, or melting ice. Martin's leak mysteriously came and went. The Friedmans couldn't walk away from that problem, and I didn't either. For several years the builder and I worked on that leak, until we finally fixed it.

But that isn't all I'd tell a prospective client. I'd suggest he or she call Martin and get his version of the leak. Ask Martin, I'd say, whether I behaved responsibly and whether he was satisfied with my work on that addition both then and now, some years later. (And let me tell you, dear reader, that once you have designed a leaky skylight for Martin Friedman, who knows how to express displeasure, you will never, ever design another skylight that leaks. And I haven't.)

Getting another client's opinion is the final test you should apply to your prospective architect. Ask for the phone numbers of two or three of his or her clients. If the architect seems uneasy about such referrals, you should feel uneasy about the architect. At the same time, remember that no one is perfect, and every architect does make mistakes. It is how the architect handles those mistakes that counts. If your prospective designer pretends that he or she *never* has made a mistake on a house and that your house will proceed without any glitches, watch to see if the designer's nose grows several inches on the spot.

Before you leave the prospective architect's office, look around. Is it distinctive? What is the special character of this environment? Is it pleasant, well lighted, colorful? What pains has the architect taken to make it livable? Do you feel comfortable in the space? Can you see some study models around (which will indicate that the architect considers every design in the third dimension)? If the architect does not work alone, make sure you know what persons have been responsible for whatever architecture you've been shown that you admired. You'll want those particular designers to work on your own house.

You might even ask if you can visit the architect's home environment at some convenient time. Some architects won't like this, because, as their wives or husbands will quickly tell you, they give more attention to their paying clients' needs than to their spouse's. But from looking at an architect's own house, you will learn a great deal about that architect's values and skills. What does he or she really care about? Someone once told me that 90 percent of lawyers do not make out their own wills. I wouldn't want one of those lawyers to make out *my* will, and I wouldn't trust an architect to design me a wonderful living space if he or she didn't live in one.

After you have interviewed your prospective architect, considered samples of work, talked with former clients, and visited some built environments, you should have a strong sense of whether the house of your dreams will be in good hands. Now you need to learn something about how you can contribute to the success of this project. When an architect and client get together, the fun—and the work—really starts.

WHEN AN ARCHITECT AND CLIENT SIT DOWN TO WORK

I've loved most of my clients. I'm not sure whether you'd hear a doctor or a lawyer say that. I'm grateful to my clients as well, for I couldn't practice my craft without them. A painter can put brush to canvas, a sculptor can mold or chisel clay or stone, and my wife, a writer, usually begins most of her stories and essays without any particular commission or even guarantee of publication. All of these artists can work without a patron. They may have a hard time eating, but they can create.

An architect, however, must have a client. An architect wants to build, and build with inspiration and with verve. Imaginary projects, or projects that will never get past the drawing board, do not satisfy most architects. Few designers are satisfied with detailed plans or even exquisitely constructed scale models. A sculptor would never be happy with only a sketch of a proposed three-dimensional work of art. Architects want to see their work, walk by and into and through it. They want others to experience its physical presence.

Over the years, I have heard some of our finest contemporary architects, from Robert A. M. Stern to Frank Gehry, lecture about their work. When even a successful and acclaimed architect, with prize-winning buildings to his or her credit, shows slides of work that never got off the drawing board—perhaps the clients changed their minds, or the board of directors couldn't raise the money, or a change of administration stopped the project cold—I can hear nostalgia in their voices, a kind of tender sadness about those unrealized plans. Only another architect can fully appreciate how they feel.

So, as a client, you can enter an architect's office with a very different emotion from the one you probably have when you visit the doctor. You seldom are led to believe that you are doing your doctor a favor or that you are enabling him or her to practice a profession. The architect, however, *wants* you; the architect *needs* you; and you are entering into what ought to be a mutually gratifying relationship.

I am prepared to think positively about a potential client right away. Each year I tell my architectural students, "One of the rewards of this very difficult and relatively low-paid profession is that architects are the best of people, equaled only by the people who hire architects, especially to design personal houses." A client who has the imagination to hire an architect, who wants a house that will not only be an adequate shelter but also a proud building and perhaps even a work of art, is probably a person with broad interests, curiosity, and artistic sensibility. If an architect has acquired over the years a reputation for designing interesting houses, his or her future clients will probably be people who are themselves interesting. Over time, an architect tends to get the clients he or she deserves.

Assuming that I'm going to like my clients does not mean I expect them to agree with me all the time or even to let me make all the decisions. Designing a house should be a collaboration that is satisfying to both parties, architect and client, and no collaboration is either easy or painless. A good client is not a pushover. I've read articles about how to be a good patient, written from a doctor's point of view, and although the doctor always urges patients to contribute to their own health care, usually by volunteering relevant information, asking questions, and following instructions, the doctor never proposes that patients suggest—even demand—definite changes in the course of treatment on the basis of an aesthetic opinion. If I told a doctor, "No, that isn't the kind of diagnosis I had in mind. I'd like something— well, I don't know, it's hard to describe—maybe a little less complicated, with fewer words but more feeling. Please work up a better one, and I'll be back next week to check it out," he'd probably call in the nearest psychiatrist for a consultation.

The first way a client can contribute to a successful project is to be as candid as possible. How big a house do you really feel you need? How much money are you prepared to spend? How open are you to a design that may be quite different from what you now have in mind? That may be different from the other houses on your block? From the kind of house your boss has? Who will make the final decision—you, your wife, or both?

When I was asked recently to design a house for a couple, the husband, who was about to leave town on business for several weeks, told me, "Louise is the conservative one. She'll be harder to please. But if she likes the design you come up with, I know I will too. I'm up to anything. Just check it with her." So I worked hard and came up with a design that not only fit their spatial requirements but had an intriguing and unusual configuration. I refined it, built a scale model, and proudly presented it to Louise, who loved it. But three weeks later, after her husband had returned, he came to see me. "You'll have to start over," he said somewhat sheepishly. "I just don't like it. It's too—I don't know, too startling. Too modern." If he had been honest with me at the beginning about who was not only the real decision-maker but also the true conservative in the family, he could have saved us both some time.

But of course I started again, and I produced another design that all three of us liked. (Which is not to say I'm not wistful about that first design, which will never be built. It was very special.) Responding to a client's intellectual and emotional nature is simply part of an architect's job.

To be a good client, you need to tell your architect as clearly and as fully as possible exactly what you want in your house. Many architects, longing for the cachet that seems to surround social scientists and psychologists, talk about "studying the life-style" of their clients in profound depth in order to decide what kind of house to design for them. Some devise elaborate questionnaires, creative games, and exercises to learn their clients' needs and desires. They practically give the client a clinical intake interview and a Rorschach test. (This admittedly has one positive effect: the client ends up feeling very important.)

I do talk at length with my clients, and I pay attention to what they tell me and to what I observe. After so many years of designing houses, I usually know what questions will elicit useful responses. Most essential facts—what we call the "program" for the building—surface surprisingly quickly.

In my experience, clients planning a house, no matter how distinctive their individual tastes, have the same fundamental desires, which they may not even have articulated to themselves. For instance, they probably want a combination of privacy and openness. In the social part of the house—the entry, living, dining, and sometimes kitchen areas—they want to be able to move easily among their guests and family members. They want to know what's happening in front of the television set, or in the conversational grouping before the fireplace.

The kitchen is now frequently one of these open spaces. As cooking has become increasingly an art as well as a necessity, the chef wants to show off a bit—but not miss any of the fun the rest of the gang are having. Yet even when the kitchen is a focal point for sociability, many people also want to be able to close off that space when they wish. During that easy, relaxed time after guests at a dinner party have just finished their meal, who wants to be staring at a stack of dirty dishes?

Most people want to have certain rooms very private. My wife was fierce about having seclusion in her study as well as our bedroom, both rooms that I planned at Wind Whistle to be somewhat apart from the main traffic pattern of the house. Most families want at least the master bedroom to be a sanctuary of quiet, and children, who are not always consulted, desperately need their private places as well. I have known a few houses designed with an open bathroom, which as far as I'm concerned brings sociability either to a new high or a new low. Thank goodness no client has ever asked me to design one!

So clients need to think about where they want to share living space and where they want to draw real or invisible—but very clear—lines of privacy. A good client will encourage the architect to achieve acoustical privacy as well. It does little good to create a separate room if sound travels freely through the walls, doors, and floors. (If you've ever tried to sleep while a teenager is having a slumber party in the room below, you'll know what I mean.) An architect can use acoustical baffling within walls and can specify other materials and details that will muffle sound.

After covering these general aspects of design, the architect and client can begin to explore the client's passions, obsessions, and pet dislikes. I always probe the depth of reasoning behind some of the client's architectural assumptions. Many of my new clients tell me, for instance, "I don't like flat roofs." I need to know *why*. Some of the most beautiful contemporary houses have flat roofs; some of the ugliest have them too. Roof lines are hard to handle; it takes skill to give grace and elegance to a flat-roofed building. Or clients may think they dislike flat roofs because they've heard that those roofs leak. This is one of modern architecture's most enduring myths. A flat roof won't leak any more readily than a pitched roof. It all depends on how the roofline is designed and how the flat roof is built. It can in fact be one of the most durable of all roof types.

As they get to know each other, the architect needs to explore the client's real range of options. What is possible or at least thinkable? A client may desperately want a brick house or dislike stucco or yearn for small-paned windows. Many people are very nervous about color. They don't want a palette that extends beyond today's fashions, which are currently white, pale yellow, or wood stains on the exterior, and perhaps a few pastels and whitewashed wood on the interior. The vogue for off-white is waning, but its legacy is a timorous attitude toward any color that sings instead of whispers.

Clients often tell me, "I like wood." They think they want wood interiors, but what do they mean? So many woods are dark, reflecting little light. Redwood and cedar, used extensively on an interior, can markedly darken a room to the point of gloom. Is this what they mean? Or do they mean woods that are naturally light, like pine, birch, or white oak, or woods that are whitewashed? Because I feel so strongly about rooms that are light inside, I will advise clients to choose the second option. In any case, "liking wood" is only a beginning.

After the first few meetings, I will be aware of most of my clients' predilections and prejudices. They will know about mine, too. At some point, they will have to decide to take what I call a "leap of faith," a phrase I use cautiously, since architects are all too often accused of godlike aspirations. To me, a leap of faith simply means that my client trusts me. This trust forms the underpinning for what becomes a complex undertaking; it is almost as important as the solid ground upon which the new house is going to be placed.

Just as a client hopes for thoughtful attention, skill, and courtesy from an architect, the architect has certain expectations of a client. A good client is reasonably available. Since I regard the design process as collaborative, I need to be able to get in touch with my client quickly, usually with a phone call. I would not like to design a house for some-one who just gave me carte blanche and left the country for six months, and when I need a fast consultation on a critical decision, I dislike having to batter down a wall of secretaries.

I've had many clients I've thought of as ideal. In Chapter 7, "The Design Process," I mention Gerald and Pat Michaelson, old friends in western Minnesota, for whom I've designed several projects. Their open-ness to an unusual idea for an outdoor shelter, an enclosed platform that became a kind of gazebo or "folly" more commonly seen on English country estates than on a Minnesota farm, made them a joy to design for. They took a leap of faith and ended up (several months later) inside a stunning small building.

Even another architect can be a superb client, though at first—given what everyone knows about architects' egos—this might seem impossible. Bernard Schober of Green Bay, Wisconsin, an architect involved primarily in the design of hospitals, and his wife, Ruth, selected our firm as their architects for a new house. It is rare for an architect to be so confident—to have so "healthy a self-image," as today's pop psychologists would put it—that he or she can say, "Another architect has more skill in this area than I do." The Schobers chose an excellent site, stated their program and budget very clearly, and kept a discerning eye on my work. Although it must often have been a temptation, Bernard never tried to prescribe specific design solutions and never handed me any little drawings he wanted me to follow. He did suggest areas that required solutions, and sometimes we worked them out together. But I never had to wrestle for control of the project.

Another Bernard, Dr. Bernard Gerber of Aberdeen, South Da-kota, represents a treasure in architectural practice, a repeat client. Twenty-five years ago, I designed his house in Aberdeen, and five projects later, I value our friendship as much as our working rela-tionship. He has on occasion been willing to wait for the right solution. Several years ago, he asked me to add a special room to his family's house, a combination of greenhouse, hot tub, and retreat. It had exacting and unique technical requirements—a climate in which he could raise orchids and bananas during fierce winters on the plains, enough natural sunlight for a greenhouse, but an environment that would not become a sauna in the heat of a Midwestern summer. I also had to locate it on the site properly and make it compatible in aesthetic terms with the existing house. Partly because I was involved in several large projects with fixed deadlines, I took a year and a half to come up with the right idea. I do not expect most of my clients to wait around for me, and I was grateful for Bernard's patience.

Enthusiasm is one of the best contributions a client can make. It is contagious, spurring an architect to ever greater efforts. I remember fondly another very pleasant commission, a house I designed for Larry and April Chang-Miller, two young doctors at the Mayo Clinic in Rochester, Minnesota. They took an equal interest in their house design, which is more satisfying (though sometimes more complicated) for an architect than just dealing with one decision-maker. Though very busy professionals, they both came to every meeting with me. If they needed to make a decision, they consulted with each other on the spot, in a clear and straightforward way, and I had an answer immediately. Just as important, Larry and April openly shared their excitement throughout the process, from our first visit to the site through every meeting afterward. When clients say, "We love the way the living room has worked out! Do you think we'll have great views from the other rooms too?" an architect rises to the occasion. Great views are practically guaranteed!

Of course every architect has memories of some clients who were not ideal. I remember a surgeon who guided my drawing hand as firmly as he might have wielded a scalpel in someone's chest. I remember a very wealthy businessman who eagerly spent twice as much for a house as the "absolute top limit" he had initially specified. (An architect designs at a particular budget level, so such upgrading is not the blessing it might appear.) I once suffered along with a battling couple who couldn't agree on anything; they divorced six months after the house was complete. I still harbor unpleasant feelings toward the client who allowed an interior decorator to "do the rooms" without any reference to the character of the house, so that the weird jumble inside utterly spoiled the design as a whole. Considering that I've designed houses for thirty-odd years, however, that is a very short list.

One particular kind of client-architect relationship is fraught with danger. That is when the client is a blood relative or a very good friend. Although this closeness *can* enhance an architect-client relationship (as with my old friends the Michaelsons, whom I mention above), it often does not. Because both parties assume they know each other well, the requisite "sorting out" doesn't take place. They don't ask enough questions, they hold back criticism in order to avoid hurt feelings, and they take comments personally.

Money can cause the greatest awkwardness between friends or relatives. Time is the architect's money, and the professional will not do his best at bargain rates. A few friends or relatives, alas, think you can do their house "on the side." (Susan likens this to a doctor who gave her the manuscript of a long novel he'd written, hoping for her advice and comments, "just when you have the time.")

During the long process of designing and building a house, goodwill and understanding on both sides will almost always prevent any real unpleasantness. I usually give my clients a standard contract developed by the American Institute of Architects (see Appendix B for a sample), whose primary purpose is to make clear our responsibilities to each other. It states the extent of my services, what they will cost, and when the costs will be due. Any extra costs will be explained on this document. Nothing in this contract will come as a surprise to my clients, because we have discussed it long before it is time to sign.

With many clients, I simply have a short letter of agreement, signed by each of us, which confirms the terms we've arranged. It is not even unusual to conduct the whole business on an oral exchange and handshake. (Susan tells me she and her New York agent, whom she has trusted implicitly for ten years, have never worried about a contract of any kind.) If a client and I have serious trouble, all the legal documents in the world will do little to resolve it. We will do much better by depending on our common sense, good will, and mutual belief in fairness. Clients who choose me do so at least partly, I hope, on my reputation as a reasonably decent and honest human being, and, as I said earlier, an architect usually gets the clients he or she deserves.

When clients sit down to work with an architect, they should feel comfortable about what lies ahead. Acting as consultant, decision-maker, and cheerleader in the process of creating a new house, the client is an essential and valued partner. It can be an enjoyable partnership that could last months or even years.

WHAT WILL IT
ALL COST?

What will your house cost? Don't be embarrassed to ask about how an architect plans to allocate your budget. After a first interview, the architect should be aware of how much you are willing to spend, but now you need to know, as closely as possible, how big a loan to discuss with your bank. If your architect is experienced, he or she should be able to give a realistic figure. Although cost is a critical issue, many people seem to feel it is somehow impolite to raise it. Perhaps they assume it is strange, mysterious, and even unknowable, a dark blur that only gets illuminated in terrible bursts of lightning, just before a storm is about to hit.

Some of us remember the hapless hero (Cary Grant at his comic best) of *Mr. Blandings Builds His Dream House,* in which cost kept rising like record-breaking floodwaters. Others have heard chilling stories about friends and friends of friends who are said to have gone nearly into bankruptcy before a house was finished, or whose marriage foundered on their growing indebtedness, or who had to abandon a half-done house because they could not afford to complete it.

Take heart. If you've chosen well, your architect should be able to tell you approximately what a house costs per square foot in your area. This means that if you want a house with acceptable but not extravagant or individually designed detail, you should expect to pay a certain amount, based on the size of the house. This cost varies, of course, with location. Here in Minneapolis in 1990, for example, I figured about $90 per square foot for an architect-designed, custom-built house with a certain complexity and some special detail. With inflation, of course, this estimate will rapidly go out of date, and anyone picking up this book in a few years will probably laugh, with a bitter undertone, at how little that $90 now sounds.

I am estimating here the cost of the kind of house that many people who can afford an architect want to build, neither a "starter" home nor a highly elaborate one. It would probably have a master bedroom, three other bedrooms, a living-dining area, a smaller family room, a kitchen, and two baths. The rooms would be ample but not grand. Although this house would not be opulent, it would have some additions and amenities that a less expensive house would lack. It might include, for example, a cathedral ceiling in one or more rooms, a roof deck, a fireplace in the master bedroom, or windows specially ordered in a particular size or shape. The preliminary estimate would look something like this:

PRELIMINARY ESTIMATE

2,400 sq. ft.@ $90	$216,000
Unfinished basement (none)	–
Garage allowance	15,000
Contingency allowance at 5%	10,950
Total construction costs	241,950
Architect's fee at 10% of above	24,195
Landscape allowance	15,000
TOTAL ESTIMATE	$281,145

One cost in this list a client may be curious about is the architect's fee. That 10 percent figure looks handsome, considered as payment for one professional's time. But it actually covers long hours by a team of architects and engineers, who coordinate a complex project. Our firm maintains an office with secretaries and equipment and employs a staff of about a dozen highly educated and trained architects, who do not earn colossal salaries, despite their advanced degrees. Architects have a much lower average yearly income than most other highly trained professionals, a fact that has an advantage for the client: architects join our profession because they really love the work.

Good design doesn't happen quickly or easily. Developing the main idea involves overseeing a multitude of parts. When we prepare our documentation, we are immersed in details. Wind Whistle, for example, needed thirteen sheets of construction drawings, including the lighting plans, and a dozen or so $8\frac{1}{2} \times 11$-inch detail sheets. Our document of specifications, which describes materials, standards of construction, and equipment, must be prepared individually for each project.

A lot of time is spent at the drafting table. Our office takes special pride in our drawings, some of which are included in this book as illustrations. Our techniques and tools are not especially elaborate—mainly pencil or paper on white or yellow tracing paper—but they do involve time. We also make three-dimensional study models, sometimes remade many times, not only to help the architect visualize the design in all its complexity but also to help our clients understand the plan. We do not expect even the most intelligent and well-educated client to be able to "read" the plans, sections, and elevations that are so clear to architects.

Much of our time also goes into meetings with clients. Later my colleagues and I spend many hours on the site, observing and expediting the process of construction. Time equals money, and time is the primary expense in an architect's fee.

If you study the preliminary estimate of costs above, you will note that this figure is not all-inclusive. It excludes the cost of the lot and of interior furnishings, both items that vary enormously. But it does cover plumbing fixtures, lighting, finished and painted walls, and heating/cooling—everything up to code and ready for the building inspector. I also allow for standard floor coverings in this estimate—wood, vinyl, tile, or carpet. If a client wants such luxuries as Italian travertine floors or inlaid wood hand-cut in exacting designs, my floor-coverings allowance would rise dramatically.

For most people, the figure I've just cited is certainly substantial. I have a very healthy respect for the work and time it has usually taken a client to acquire enough money to invest in a custom-designed, custom-built house. Beware of an architect who regards money as insignificant or who talks of six-figure sums as if they were poker chips of different colors.

Of course, the costs of a house can rise almost without end to the height of desire—if the client has the budget to match his or her dreams. A house is a little bit like a car: some people are willing to pay for items that may not be strictly necessary, custom colors, a sunroof, four-way stereo, leather seats, a car phone. Asking "How much does a house cost?" is as open-ended as asking "How much does a car cost?" Yet most people still know the average cost for a standard high-quality car, and they realize that a top-of-the-line Porsche costs a lot more.

What does a figure higher than $90 per square foot buy? For upwards of $200 per square foot, a client can get, for example, walnut or rosewood millwork ("millwork" means the wood-crafted parts of a house, such as kitchen cabinets, bookshelves, storage space, and moldings). A client can also specify specially cast bronze door hardware, a marble fireplace, hand-designed and hand-fired ceramic tile, light fixtures that are works of art, and an abundance of careful hand craftsmanship in other details.

Custom-designed, custom-built millwork is one of the quickest ways to drive up that square-foot cost. Everyone wants some of it in an architect-designed house—perhaps oak bookshelves, a built-in sewing center, a hi-fi or television enclosure in the bedroom, a serving buffet in the dining room, or the kind of sumptuous Scandinavian kitchen cabinets that appear in magazine ads—but not everyone needs to double the cost of a house to get what he or she wants. Most of the cabinets I include in my houses are made to my specifications in local millwork shops; they are more expensive than those sold in building-supply warehouses, but they are perhaps one-third of the cost of those in the glossy advertisements.

Sometimes inexpensive, mass-produced millwork will fill the bill just fine. At Wind Whistle, I ordered some handsome white plastic-laminate kitchen cabinets with natural oak edging. Their inner edges are a bit rough, but they are sturdy, durable, and good-looking, and they cost half the price of custom cabinets (and a quarter the price of European imports). An architect keeps an eye open for such finds, and he or she should have a ready file of information for clients to explore.

Is it possible to have an architect-designed, custom-built house for $75 a square foot? Yes, although that would probably be (in 1990) the minimum. In a $75-a-foot house, the construction would be absolutely sound, and the design would still be of high quality. The house would not have as much volume; for instance, one room might have some height to it rather than several. The configuration of the plan would be simple and easy to frame and to roof. It would be a compact house, probably several stories high, in order to minimize the roof surface and the foundation work. The architect would omit almost all of the custom-designed detail that requires significant hand labor. Almost everything would be ready-made and "off the rack."

"Off the rack" does not need to be shoddy or unattractive. The architect simply has to be more diligent in searching out the right items. (The kitchen cabinets I mentioned above are a good example.) Plain red-oak floors are not expensive, and they are both serviceable and handsome. The common Luxo lamp, or "architect's lamp," is a functional, streamlined, and inexpensive light fixture. We use several in our own house, as desk lamps in our study and as reading lights attached to small built-in shelves next to our beds. Plastic laminate can be a relatively inexpensive, but very colorful, surface finish. At Wind Whistle, my wife's desk and computer station is covered in a pale pink laminate that complements the rosy-pink stained wood of the ceiling. She thinks it is an ideal work surface, sleek and easily cleaned.

An architect can help with other cost-cutting measures, suggesting, for example, single-layer Sheetrock (the material used for most modern walls) rather than double. Double, of course, has its advantages—it provides better sound insulation and is less subject to nail-popping—but single will look just as good, at least initially. The client may also elect to have only two coats of paint rather than three on walls, doors, and millwork; this is another decision weighing long-term durability against economy. If you plan to be easy on your surfaces—no small feet kicking the walls, no constant changing and rehanging of pictures, no muddy paw prints on the doors— two coats of paint may be fine.

As for exterior materials, an economical plan may use textured plywood rather than clear redwood or cedar siding. "Textured plywood" sounds worse than it is. At first glance, it has the same surface as solid wood (though on second glance, it looks like a fake); it is durable, and it can be stained for color. Redwood siding can be used more economically by leaving it to weather naturally, rather than giving it a three-coat paint job. Roofing in a more expensive house might be slate, tile, or cedar shingles; in a less expensive house, I would use asphalt shingles. They come in different colors and textures, and if used properly, they provide sound roofs and are actually rather unobtrusive.

When I present my initial cost estimate to my clients, I carefully explain what it means and what the choices have been. They may want to modify those choices, substituting one cost-saving measure for another.

The estimate is not a guarantee. I stress this statement, because an architect-client relationship can founder on it. At this point in the process, the estimate is an educated guess. That is why a client might do well to work with an architect who has had years of on-the-job education. Only after continued development of the design can the figures be refined further.

I try to make this estimate absolutely realistic—for somewhat selfish reasons. If I am wrong, and the costs are much higher, I will have to redo my design in order to make the costs conform to the client's budget. Since (as noted early in this section) my fee is a percentage of the total budget and not an hourly rate of pay, I would lose money if I had to spend more time on the design. I want to get it right at the beginning.

Staying within the budget, then, is in my interest. It is also in my interest to make sure my clients have given me a figure that represents their *actual* budget, neither a lower budget they'd like to get away with but can easily exceed if necessary nor an upper fantasy budget they can never reach. Together we need to arrive at an accurate budget and plan within it. On this question of costs, I am on *their* side.

Not long ago, in the process of preparing final plans for a house that would soon go out for bids, two clients visited my office with their interior decorator. The decorator, whom I'll call George, went over the plans with me. He urged my clients to substitute a different type of kitchen cabinets for the ones we had selected. I agreed that his chosen cabinets were indeed superb in quality and very luxurious-looking, the Mercedes of the kitchen-cabinet field, but they were also very expensive. The change would have added some thousands of dollars to an already tight budget. I urged the clients to stay with the less expensive, and perfectly acceptable, cabinets. George looked at me rather scornfully. How could I, an architect, not want to join him in recommending a more elegant interior detail? "Whose side are you on, anyway?" he asked in disbelief. If I'd been his clients, I think I'd have fired George on the spot.

After my clients and I agree on a basic plan and a preliminary estimate, I begin "design development," a process of refining the design and making everything in it much more specific. At this stage, I select materials and clarify details. If we have decided on wood siding as an exterior material, for example, I now choose what kind of wood, what type of boards (horizontal or vertical), tongue-and-groove or wood battens, painted, stained, or natural, and so on. In this process, I am thinking often about the client's budget. If we are planning wood floors, I will know whether the budget allows teak or dictates oak. After all these decisions, I then have a "preliminary specification," with many more accompanying drawings.

Now I am ready to confer with a builder on costs. This is not the actual bidding process, but a preliminary stage when I want to find out how much house we can buy with a client's budget. I pick a builder (or contractor; these are professional labels I use interchangeably) I have worked with before, so I know how he or she performs on the job. I make sure this particular builder is appropriate for this size of house (a single carpenter, working more or less alone, would not be the best one to figure costs for a six-bedroom, three-bath, four-level house). I will pay the builder (from my own fee) for the time it takes to figure this more detailed cost estimate. The second estimate might be as follows, taken from an actual project bid out in

November 1989, a house with about 3,000 square feet of finished space:

COST ESTIMATE AT COMPLETION OF DESIGN DEVELOPMENT

Setup expenses	$3,500
Site work	3,900
Concrete/masonry	8,800
Materials	77,000
Carpentry labor	37,800
HVAC (heating, ventilating, air conditioning)	9,400
Plumbing	10,800
Electrical	9,800
Exterior finishes	900
Wall finishes	7,200
Floor finishes	13,000
Painting and decorating	6,900
Finish and bath hardware	3,500
Contractor's overhead & profit	22,135
Miscellaneous	2,500
This total is for building construction:	271,135
Now add a contingency fund at 5%	13,557
	284,692
Now add 10% of this sum for architect's fee	28,469
Add landscape allowance at	15,000
The total of this estimate will be	$328,161

If the final estimate is within the client's range, our firm will complete the construction drawings and specifications. These form the package that allows builders to submit a price with the secure knowledge that they are all bidding on exactly the same product. Then we put the house out to bids from contractors.

At this point the client and I can follow several different paths. The most common is to ask three or four selected contractors to submit a fixed, lump-sum price to complete the work outlined in the bid package. Another path is to choose a single contractor whom the architect or owner or both trust completely; architect and contractor together work out the fixed, lump-sum price. As the contractor then gets bids from his or her subcontractors (those who supply building materials, electrical, heating/cooling, plumbing, roofing, etc.), the contractor and I and sometimes the owner can confer and alter or refine our choices if necessary. In both of these alternatives, *the builder is bound to fulfill his or her obligations for the fixed sum agreed*, unless changes are made.

Unlikely as it sounds, I am just as wary of a contractor who substantially underbids a job as I am of one who overbids. I have more than once advised an owner to accept a bid that wasn't the bottom one submitted. I want to see a bid that is realistic, one that will allow the contractor to do a good job for an honest profit, because otherwise, trouble lies ahead. Nothing can be more disastrous to a finished house than a contractor who is losing money on his or her work. The contractor may cut corners on essential details, skimp on materials, and hold up delivery on supplies if he or she can't pay suppliers. The contractor's psyche will understandably be suffering, too; sinking deeper into debt each day, he or she will sour on the whole project. Underbidding can also be a cue that the contractor is inexperienced, another warning of problems down the line.

Obviously, most clients are going to be attracted to a fixed-sum agreement. They know they won't have to worry about significant cost overruns. But I (and sometimes my clients) have often followed a third path, the one I used to my satisfaction when building Wind Whistle. This involves working with only one contractor in developing and refining an estimate, but then not holding the contractor to a fixed-sum agreement. Instead, as the owner, I take responsibility for the final costs. The contractor does not have to worry that he or she will be putting in time or materials that will not be paid for. The owner and architect in turn have the flexibility to make adjustments as building proceeds.

This procedure probably sounds dangerous. What if the contractor wastes time? What about featherbedding, careless use of materials, and sloppy work? Earlier, in talking about how to select and work with an architect, I spoke about the client's need to take a "leap of faith." I take the same leap with contractors. I would never hire on this basis a contractor whom I did not absolutely trust. This contractor also will want me to recommend him or her for other jobs, and a good reputation is an invaluable business asset.

What are the advantages of this arrangement? By not asking the contractor to take a significant financial risk, I free him or her from unduly worrying about costs. So, when the contractor figures an estimate, he or she doesn't need to pad it to protect against financial loss. Also, the contractor will be as meticulous in detail and finishing as I would wish. With a fixed-sum bid, cost constraint may drive the project more than quality.

At Wind Whistle, since my builders, Larry Smith and Mark Vogen, didn't need all the specifications for a firm bid, I felt comfortable getting started on the building of the house before I had developed every detail. As we went along, they were able to complete each phase to my absolute satisfaction. The complex geometry of the roof, for example, required much handcrafting, and the work took longer than anyone thought it would, but I received full value from the cost of the extra time involved. When I peer over the railing on our crow's-nest balcony, I can see how carefully the wood shingles are overlapped at the peaks, each one cut to a precise angle. I got a meticulous fit for both appearance and longevity. Not only will the roof be watertight, but it is a masterpiece of woodworker's art.

If I had been the architect for another owner, not myself, we would have discussed the roof, its detailing, and its costs together. It is certainly possible we might have decided on some other alternatives in design or construction, though none would have had the same combination of elegance and long-term economy. During every aspect of designing and building a house, an architect spends many, many hours juggling between desires and budget realities. Owners must often help decide about options, since it is, after all, their house. Yet I care about the house, too. I want it to be a fine example of my own art. When a client and an architect get together and work out the final plans for a house that will be both wonderful and affordable, we are indeed on the same side.

THE SITE: WHERE WILL IT GO?

In order to build a house, you have to have something to build it on. For most people, the process of planning a house begins with choosing a site: a city lot, suburban acreage, a piece of land in the country. Sometimes an architect may help the client choose the best place for a particular dream house, but almost always the lot comes first. People may hold that lot for years, walking over every inch of it season by season, studying its contours and vegetation, dreaming about where one day they'll put the living room, or a playhouse, or a garden. Or they may buy a lot one sudden day and decide almost immediately to begin to build. In either case, the owners will probably love that bit of land and want a house that takes full advantage of it.

That is where the architect will begin, too: studying the site and trying to take full advantage of it. An architect should spend considerable time on a "site study." This professional-sounding term simply means putting down on paper and perhaps even in a three-dimensional model all the relevant facts about the site. The site study should make each element clear, and the client should be able to see everything on it as easily as the architect.

The site study includes site gradient (where and how much the lot deviates from the level); major trees; neighbors, if any; views, if any; sun angles, winter and summer; types of soil, if they may present problems; and potential visual or aural distractions, such as highways or neighborhood structures. Conventional architectural wisdom dictates "prevailing winds" as part of the site study, but since modern construction techniques make a house so closed and tight, I no longer usually find this an essential element. What *is* essential is committing everything else I've mentioned to paper. Too often my architectural students—and even practicing architects—try to carry all those facts in their heads, and some of the data disappears.

Site often has a greater impact on design than any other single factor. Every site is unique, with its own advantages and problems. *Every* site has its strong points. If a designer deals with site issues in a creative and responsible way, he or she will already have earned the architect's fee.

First an architect must consider the context of the site: its neighborhood, city, and region. That context will indicate, among other directives, climate, tradition, construction techniques and materials, and a whole range of aesthetic variables. In Minnesota, for example, I would be crazy to build a house encircling an outdoor lanai. Swiss chalets look and feel marvelous in the Alps, but when I see one in southern California, it looks pretty silly to me. Exposed concrete, especially if painted, is fine among the balmy foliage of Florida, but in Maine it would be cold and uninviting. Stucco on a sloped or raked wall works in Arizona, but in any freezing climate, it soon deteriorates, since water runs off a vertical wall but penetrates a slope.

Evaluating the neighborhood of a site, an architect must consider scale. Architects use the word "scale" a lot, talking about whether a building is "in scale" or "out of scale," either to describe the relationship of the size of a house to its neighbors or to humans. A house or a living room may be "out of scale," too large or too high. A clever architect, however, can make some adjustments in design to compensate for scale. If a house will be much larger than its neighbors, a designer needs to use some aesthetic camouflage (unless the owner wants a house that will shout and stamp its feet.)

One of my clients wanted and needed a large house in a neighborhood he loved, which had rather small city lots and modest one-story houses. So I designed his house with four modules or "pods" connected by enclosed short walkways. Each pod contained a logical grouping of functions, such as kitchen/dining/family or living room/master bedroom or children's bedrooms. The steep roofs of the one-story house made it an integrated composition. Now the finished house lies on the lot in such a way that only one or two parts show up from any single vantage point. It is an unobtrusive "good neighbor."

On another city lot, I designed for a single person a house that was much smaller than the older, substantial family homes in the neighborhood. I did not want it to look out of scale, in this case meaning "dinky." So I planned a small "footprint" (the outline of the house if drawn as it sits on the ground) but built it vertically on several levels, so it matched in scale the height of its next-door neighbors. Later, when the single owner married, I had room to add a substantial wing to the footprint, so the house eventually matched the bulk of its neighbors.

If a neighborhood has a particular predominant style, an architect must take this into account. This does not mean that he or she must design in the same style, creating, for example, a fake English Tudor to match the other 1920s or 1930s stucco-and-wood houses. But a good designer can acknowledge the prevalent style in terms of color, scale, materials, and details, so that a new house adapts to its surroundings without sacrificing its contemporaneity and individuality. Of course, some architects (and owners) want to use a new house to thumb their noses at their benighted and bourgeois neighbors. I'm not sure how happy those owners are in the neighborhood after they've moved in. In such a case, I know I wouldn't want to leave my house on Halloween night.

Aside from the actual design, building a house in an existing neighborhood sometimes creates a delicate public-relations problem. The whole neighborhood often feels a certain proprietary interest in a vacant lot, which gives them a little additional open space, almost like a private park. When that vacant lot disappears, turning into a house, everyone looks on that change with a certain suspicion and occasionally downright hostility. If the owner wants a design with some special qualities—"modern" is a frightening word to a lot of people—that hostility may become quite overt. When the architect walks around the site, studying it, he or she in turn feels the presence of inquisitive eyes behind neighboring curtains or blinds.

I remember vividly my first encounter of this kind, even though it took place thirty years ago. I had walked onto a small urban site between two houses, and I was busily pounding stakes into the ground, trying out different locations for my house. Soon I was joined by one of the neighbors next door. She looked at me fiercely and said, "You're not planning to build on this lot, are you?" I was young, and not terribly tactful, and I'm afraid I responded just as vigorously. "Yes, I certainly am," I told her. Soon we found ourselves close to argument, as she pleaded with me to leave this lot alone, and I (having sunk our family savings into this ground) refused to back down. Although I did try to reassure her that my design would do its best to respect her view, I knew that her living room looked directly over and into the very—and only—spot where my new house could and would go. Although I did avoid any windows that looked into hers, I built my house as planned. We were never too fond of each other after that.

Just eight years ago, I built myself another house. Although I again chose an urban lot, small and difficult enough to have been overlooked for years, but situated in a lovely, old, traditional neighborhood, I had learned something about diplomacy. When the lady from next door appeared on my lot and asked if I was going to build a house, I told her yes, and that I knew she would really like what I had in mind. When my schematic design was complete, I took both drawings and a scale model and showed them to my immediate neighbors on both sides. I wanted them to know just what I was planning. I had considered the design of their houses, and I explained to them how my very contemporary house would fit in and why the design was logical and right. They soon accepted the house with grace, and now I think they are even proud of it as an interesting addition to the neighborhood.

After studying the neighborhood and its larger context, the architect turns his or her attention to what we might call the geology of the site. The most important feature to consider is often the gradient, or slope, of the land. Although a flat site is easy to plan for, it may sometimes be a rather dull environment within which to place a house, especially if it has no trees. A sloping site, though offering difficulties, also creates some striking opportunities for design.

The most problematical slope is one that rises directly up from the street, since setback requirements (the legal distance a building must be set back from the street) mean that the house will virtually sit on top of a hill. Not only is it hard to place a garage in the right spot in order to avoid a steep driveway, which will be a disaster in seasons of ice, snow, and sleet, but digging into the hill may mean denuding the lot of its trees. Sometimes I can respond to this kind of site by locating the living levels one or even two stories above the garage. Although the entry is obviously rather removed from the street, the house then does often compensate with enhanced views. Most of the time, however, I prefer to disturb the natural grade of the land as little as possible.

Whenever a site has handsome trees, I regard them as a design imperative: DO NOT DESTROY. Cherish and guard your trees! They cannot be easily replaced, at least not for more years than most owners want (or are able!) to wait. So, except for those trees that absolutely must go to make room for the house or driveway or planned garden, I do not want to cut them down. Not only are they beautiful elements of nature, but they provide shade and soften and frame the architecture.

As I make a site plan, I try to locate all the major trees and note their size and type. In my design for the house and drive, I want to enhance those trees and use them as part of my landscape plan. You can change the grade only minimally around existing trees, or they will slowly but surely die. Of course, if you are building within a dense stand of trees, you will have to make some careful pruning decisions in order to allow adequate sun and light into your house. But be careful! Think and wait, rather than find yourself staring regretfully at an ugly, shadeless, barren stump.

Other natural features, such as rock outcroppings or particular soil conditions, should appear on a site study as well. With careful design, an architect can plan around many such conditions, like poor soil, in order to avoid the expense of substantial site work by heavy machinery.

Studying the sunlight at different times of day (and knowing how that light will differ in summer and winter) will of course help an architect plan a house for efficient use of energy. With almost everyone today aware of high costs and dwindling resources, an architect more than ever needs to coordinate design with natural factors that can help conserve energy.

Earth-sheltered or underground houses, a trend now losing its initial excitement of novelty, seem to me vastly overrated, and I do not design them. Many are half-buried shelters with shaggy grass growing in uneven patches on the dirt roof, reminiscent of the sod shelters many of our pioneer ancestors uncomfortably endured before they had time, money, or materials for better houses. Despite its attempt to blend into nature, such a house usually looks out of place in its surroundings, neither a recognizable feature of the landscape, like a mound or a tree, nor a simple but proud human structure, like a cabin or a tipi.

Such contemporary underground or heavily earth-sheltered houses have many potential problems. They need ventilation, both for comfort and to conform to codes. More important, they need light. Most humans do not want to live like moles. In order to achieve enough light and ventilation, the designer of such houses has to consider technical issues first. The plan must arrange rooms to achieve light or height or windows, rather than to suit a family's life-style, daily patterns, or circulation. That is the reverse of the design process I prefer to follow.

An underground or earth-sheltered home often causes more devastation to the site than a more conventional house, for a great deal of earth must be scooped out to make room for the structure. Underground water can seep in all too easily. I know one Minnesota house, marvelous in concept, that was literally built into a magnificent rock outcropping. Rocks jutted into the living room (somewhat as in Frank Lloyd Wright's well-known but not very livable house Falling Water), and in the first spring, rivulets of water gently coursed down the rocks into the living space. Insect life also flourishes underground, and many insects will happily make your house their home.

Finally, the alleged advantage of an earth-sheltered home, its superior insulation, is usually based on fallacious reasoning. Earth is not, in fact, a particularly good insulator. It would take seven feet of earth to do the equivalent job of twelve inches of good commercial insulation.

Some of my clients ask me about "passive solar" and "active solar" houses. In fact, good architects have always considered solar energy in designing their houses, from the days of the ancient Egyptians to the present. Sunlight is an essential factor in design, whether one wants to shield a space from too much heat or to welcome it into a cold room, or both, depending on the season. One of the virtues of a contemporary house (rather than a "period" style) is that it can better accommodate adjustment to the influence of sunlight.

"Active solar" houses usually use mechanical devices for collecting and storing sunlight, most often either in liquid or in masonry materials. Many owners who try these devices are disappointed, not only by the way design has to be skewed, but by rooms that may end up too hot or too crowded. Most architects and engineers today who are active in designing energy-efficient buildings agree that "solar" is a misleading and often misused word. My colleague Professor Lance Lavine, who is deeply involved with the Minnesota Cold Climate Building Research Center, says that the solution is a simple and old-fashioned one: insulate, insulate, insulate.

So although I will study the sunlight on a site very carefully, I will not design a house based solely on that factor. Instead, I will take the site study back to my office, consider all the complications and advantages that the site offers, and try to create a house that will become a useful, worthy, and attractive part of the landscape around it.

WHO'S HOLDING THE PENCIL?

Before an architect lifts a pencil to make the first line for the first sketch of a house, he or she is predisposed to a certain approach to architecture. I always find it hard to explain in a few words just what my approach is, and, fortunately, few clients want to discuss modernism and postmodernism, Gropius and Wright, Richard Rogers and I. M. Pei. But if I am going to give an honest account of how I approach design, perhaps I should describe what has influenced me, briefly including where I've studied, professors I've admired, architects I've worked for, travel, and books.

I entered the profession as a kind of fluke with a happy-go-lucky guess. After World War II, I enrolled at the University of Minnesota under the G.I. Bill and began to major in civil engineering. That was a short and grim venture. My roommate seemed to be having more fun. He was majoring in architecture, which seemed quite romantic, with all-night "charrettes," paper models, colored pencils, and splashy watercolors. I thought I'd give architecture a try. Once I did, I was hooked.

At Minnesota's School of Architecture in the late 1940s and 1950s, students simply breathed in modernism. It was in the air, unquestioned and pervasive. The battle had been won against traditionalists, the Beaux Arts school who worked with classical elements in time-honored designs. As students, we admired modernists like Walter Gropius, Marcel Breuer, Ludwig Mies van der Rohe, and other Bauhaus architects. Although Frank Lloyd Wright was still around, we didn't give him much credibility, because he wasn't a true modernist.

What did modernism mean to me? Then and now, I have never been caught up with pure architectural theory, at least as it is expressed in words. I didn't get a creed from books, I mainly got it from buildings. I absorbed what was essentially a rationalist approach to design, in which everything happened for a reason. Buildings expressed their structure and their use. Functionalism was king; buildings could appear to be machine-made and still be beautiful. Any material was acceptable as long as it was not made to look like something else. Some of the precepts of modernism are now clichés, but then I thought of them as cutting insights: "Form follows function," for example, or "God is in the details."

Ornaments? Pilasters, columns, cornices, swags, and swirls—all were proscribed. In our classroom design problems, a sure way to fail was to use applied ornamentation. Color? There was just one: white.

As I look over my current work now, in the 1990s, I can see how far I've come from such rigidity. I have learned to use and enjoy color, I indulge in occasional whimsy, and I am not above a little ornamentation here and there. Postmodernism, and other flurries of architectural fashion, have liberated us all from constraints that had become too restricting. A purist would look at Wind Whistle—with its vivid palette, rough-sawn ornamental beams, and judicious use of wallpaper—and flinch. (A few of my stanchly modernist friends have done that!) I may have strayed, but my heart still belongs to modernism, with its insistence on integrity, functional design, and imaginative use of spatial forms.

As a student at Minnesota, I did not "learn modernism," as if it were a text. I learned the process of design and how to complete it with skilled drawings. A few students enter architectural school with "a natural hand," an innate skill at drawing anything—a human figure, a still life, a scene. Most of us, including me, have to be taught how to depict something on paper so it is understandable. An architect's language is primarily drawing, expressing in a graphic form his or her ideas about volume, shape, size, and everything else that makes up a three-dimensional building.

Even today, in this era of computers, most of the human energy in an architectural office goes into various kinds of drawings, from sketches to the kind of complete documentation illustrated in Part Two of this book. Freehand sketches are only part of these drawings; others involve hard-line pencil drawings, made with precision instruments like T squares and triangles. Almost all these drawing skills can be acquired; mostly they take practice. At Minnesota, we practiced and practiced—and practiced.

It was at Minnesota that I met one of the first of my important mentors, Robert Cerny, a fine modernist architect who also was a fine teacher, and who provided a role model for combining those two careers. Bob Cerny taught in a practical and pithy way, and some of his directives have stuck with me all these years: "It is important for a building to have a service entrance as well as a great front door!" "A nice design, but can you put a roof on it?" "You're hired for your design ability, but you'll be rehired if the mechanical system works."

Cerny (as students referred to him, using his last name as an affectionate but respectful moniker) also taught me something about style. I came from a small town in western Minnesota, and for years I dressed as if I might have to head out to the fields at any moment. When, after graduate school, I returned to teach at Minnesota, I was still somewhat in awe of Cerny, even though we were now colleagues. And Cerny still felt, rightly, that he had something to teach me. One day he called me into his office. "Jim, you want to be a great architect, don't you?" I nodded. "You don't want anything to foul you up, do you?" I shook my head. "Well, you'd better get some of the nonessentials out of the way. Then you can concentrate on the really important stuff. So for heaven's sake, buy yourself a tie, get rid of those white socks, and throw those goddamn boots in the trash can!"

I was proud, independent, and more than a little stubborn. It took me six years to get rid of those thick-soled boots, and even then I only traded them in for black athletic shoes! Eventually I did start dressing up, in my own way, but instead of a tie, I became attached to a set of silver Native American beads. Cerny, who died in 1985, might even have liked them.

Cerny also gave me a push toward the Graduate School of Design at Harvard, my next significant academic experience. After graduating with a B. Arch. in 1952 from Minnesota and working in a dull architectural office, with few interesting projects, I became restless. I decided I needed some more training, so I went to Cerny and asked him where I ought to go. "Harvard, of course," he said. "Why?" I asked. Cerny looked at me as if I were an idiot. He grabbed a piece of paper and, like any architect under stress, made a drawing. Fiercely, with huge letters, he wrote in rough strokes on the page: H A R V A R D. As he wrote, he sounded out each letter with emphasis. Then he turned the sheet around to me and pointed to the letters. It was clear to me that the name alone, with all its implicit power and reputation, ought to grab me. It did.

Cerny may have been an extreme partisan, but he was right about Harvard. In the early 1950s—I earned my M. Arch. there in 1954—it was an exciting place. My dream had been to study with Walter Gropius, who had left Harvard the year before I came, but I was very conscious of his legacy. In fact, Gropius's graduate dormitories at Harvard still seem to me among the best modernist buildings, with their disciplined forms, crisp details, sympathetic use of outdoor space, and inclusion of work by major contemporary artists. He was succeeded by José Sert, also an impressive teacher as well as architect.

Although I had seen something of Europe when I'd served in World War II, I was still a young man from Dawson, Minnesota, when I moved to Cambridge. There I was immersed for the first time in an entirely different culture, with its own special dynamics. My friends at the time were all students at either MIT or Harvard, and we talked architecture nonstop, comparing ideas and projects and looking at buildings. We traveled to New York or New Haven or wherever within range we felt there was something compelling to see.

For many years after I moved back to Minnesota, a group of us who were mostly Cambridge-trained and Minnesota-based made an annual pilgrimage back East just to look at what was happening. John Rauma, Bruce Abrahamson, Leonard Parker, Hugh Peacock (an Englishman trained at the Architectural Association), and I would fly to Boston, rent a car, and drive up and down the East Coast, looking at buildings, admiring, criticizing, and arguing with each other. We sought out the new work of Paul Rudolph, Eero Saarinen, Louis Kahn, José Sert, the Architects Collaborative, Skidmore, Owings & Merrill, and others who were then designing significant modernist buildings. We had a great time, as architects almost always do when they get together for something other than a competitive interview!

While I was at Harvard, I found another important mentor. Working as a student in the office of Carl Koch & Associates, I saw for the first time architects who worked at a problem until they got it right. Many an architect running an office will say, "Okay, you have sixty hours to spend on this, and that's it." Whatever you accomplish in those sixty hours is what you use. But Carl and his associates showed me, by precept and example, that design involved a careful and patient search.

They always wanted to look at a number of contributory ideas. And they never gave up. Carl was sure the right answer was somewhere out there. His example has been central in my own professional life. I try to remember: Don't give up until you get it right!

In all seven years of academic architectural training, I never designed one house. Then, in the next six years of working for other architects, I was part of a team on only one, Koch's mass-produced Techbilt house. But during those years of apprenticeship, I learned my trade, as every young architect must, and the skills and knowledge I acquired then go into every house I do now. I learned how buildings actually are put together, something I could not witness at first hand during classes and design studios. I saw how the design team involved mechanical and electrical engineers, specification writers, draftspeople, the project designer, the project manager, the job captain, and the construction supervisor. Overseeing and coordinating all these people was the architect in charge.

As an apprentice architect, I often felt that the process chipped away at my basic concept until there was nothing left. (If the architect in charge does not inspire passion and conviction among his or her staff, that erosion is usually inevitable.) So I became determined that when I had my own office, I would never let others do the design without my input, and I would never let the process pass from one stage to another without participating. That is one reason (aside from economics!) I have a relatively small office; I can always keep "hands on" a project from start to finish.

Although for my thirteen years of academic training and apprenticeship I was not effectively involved in house design, I did design and build one small house for myself while I was in school (I mention this not very exciting house in my introduction). I do not count that as a mature design project. Soon after I had opened my own office, I designed another house for myself and my growing family. This one was featured in *Architectural Record*, a professional journal, and soon afterward I designed a really spectacular small house for a client, which became one of the twenty *Architectural Record* Homes of the Year, and which also appeared in a popular house-and-home magazine.

Few architects specialize in home design alone. If they did, their creativity might stagnate. Working on houses is, in fact, not so different from working on churches, schools, and other kinds of buildings. In school, in apprenticeship, and in independent practice, an architect learns the same design process: identify the problem and figure out how to solve it; establish goals, and set about achieving them. During the past year, my office designed three houses, but we were also busy with three large urban parking/transit structures, a recreation and re-habilitation camp for the physically impaired, a swim center at the University of Minnesota, and Susan's and my small garden house at Wind Whistle.

One of the most meaningful influences on my house designs has been travel. After I began studying architecture, I realized how much I had yet to see and learn. In 1945, when I was a very young lieutenant, just two years out of high school, I stood in the shadow of Rheims Cathedral. It was a hot summer day, and I shared a bottle of cham-pagne with a buddy. Unbelievable as it seems to me now, I never went inside! Several years later, after I'd finished my architectural training, Rheims was one of the first places I was determined to visit in Europe.

The Beaux Arts approach to education dictated a Grand Tour of Europe as a finishing touch. For an architect, travel is still an essential component to education. I was fortunate enough to win the Rotch Trav-eling Scholarship soon after I left Harvard, which gave me a year tour-ing around western Europe. I sought out and studied the great architectural monuments of the past as well as contemporary build-ings. It was an ever-changing feast, from new housing in Scandinavia to Michelangelo's dome at St. Peter's in Rome, from the rebuilding of postwar London to the dizzying compositions of Gaudí in Spain. While I'm sure I acquired some historical sense and some new ideas, I also know the experience greatly raised my goals as an architect. Even if I could never reach such exalted company, I wanted to stretch as far as I could.

Looking at built architecture has been the most powerful way I have continued to grow and change as a designer. I do read architectural books, but I more often study pictures than peruse the text. The text often seems boring in comparison. A few books do hold my attention all through, such as a recent study of Norman Foster's Hong Kong Bank, or a complete documentation of Hugh Newell Jacobsen's work. I study the major architectural magazines—*Architecture*, *Architectural Record*, *Progressive Architecture*, and the British magazine *Architectural Review* —not only because I like to see what contemporary architects are doing, but because these magazines use pictures as much as words.

I love to read, but I hate reading abstract theory. Not long ago, a teaching colleague urged me to have a more thoroughgoing theoretical basis for my class in design. He asked me, somewhat accusingly, "Okay, James, what was the last book you read?" I only had to think for a moment before I answered, "*Pride and Prejudice*, for the fifth time!"

Who is to say that *Pride and Prejudice*, with its humor, leisurely pace, and prose that always seems exactly right, doesn't influence me when I sit down at my drafting table? Everything I see, hear, think about, or feel probably goes into my buildings. If you ask an architect "What *kind* of designer are you?", beware of the man or woman who has an easy answer. Whoever is holding the pencil has a complicated personal, academic, and professional history.

THE DESIGN PROCESS

When Susan asked me, "How do you get your first idea? The one you put down on paper the first time?" I couldn't give her a clear answer. I can describe some of the rational criteria that help determine a design, and I can show how I change and refine a design once I have drawn it on paper. (I do this in Chapter 12, "Getting Started," where I explain my different ideas for the form and plan of Wind Whistle.) But defining the source of inspiration is not so easy. I muttered something about "magic" to Susan, and since she is a writer, I think she forgave me.

Creativity is hard to define, and perhaps impossible to teach. When I meet a new class of design students, I know that not all of them will turn out to be gifted practitioners of the art. Perhaps one or two may become nationally or internationally known for their creative architecture. Others will be capable, competent, even superior architects. I can teach all of them about basic assumptions, theoretical and practical considerations, techniques, tools, and tricks of the trade. But I can only prod the creative instinct into life and nurture it if the seed is there.

Even the phrase "design process" makes me uneasy, because it implies a logical step-by-step sequence that leads directly to the Design. Any artist, or indeed anyone engaged in creative work, knows that the final product cannot be programmed. For me, the process never goes from beginning to end in a straight line. Like a stream, it meanders all over the place. Talking to my students, I have sometimes likened it to a spiral that starts with a big loop and ultimately zeroes in on an idea. Like most working architects, I am more comfortable describing it with a pencil than with words:

I can fairly easily explain what leads up to the moment I begin to draw my first tentative images. Just as Susan tells me she has always done some "prewriting" in her head, as she is gardening or folding clothes or staring out the bedroom window, I've been pondering the design problem. From chapters 2 and 3, "How to Select an Architect" and "When an Architect and Client Sit Down to Work," you can already guess what I've been thinking about.

First are my impressions of the client. What are the passions that drive them? What do I sense about their personalities, their spirits? If a couple are involved, where are their desires and tastes alike, and where do they differ? Can I count on both of them to express themselves clearly and honestly? Is one of them the primary decision-maker? Do they have any hidden agendas? Even if I don't hear their answers in so many words, after a few meetings I have a sense of where my clients stand and who they are.

I'm not going to begin to think of a radically dramatic design for someone who has expressed nervousness about "modern architecture." I won't come up with an interior featuring a lot of glass for a woman who dreams of a cozy, introverted environment. A man who has a cool personality, who prides himself upon sophistication and sleekness, probably won't want romantic touches. One couple—informed, sensitive, and easy to work with—saved me a lot of time by declaring at one of our first meetings, "Our taste development stopped with the Bauhaus." No postmodern whimsy for them!

My clients and I need to agree upon certain essential information. Architects call this the "program": the budget, the size of the house, and the type of rooms required. If a wife wants a large house and the husband prefers a smaller one to which they might add later, I need to help them resolve some critical issues.

Before beginning a design, I have had several visits to the site. (See Chapter 5 for an overview of some of the things I look for.) I walk it at different times of the day to gauge the different kinds of light and their effects. Although I will undoubtedly visit the site at least once with the owners, I also make sure I have some time there alone. I make a site diagram (Figure 1) to keep all the issues clear and in front of me.

But my impressions, my intuitive response to the site, are just as important as all the factual material I gather. When designing a house for one couple, I stood for the first time on their lot and found myself on the lower part of a hill, which slopes gently down a long wide view to the north and west, and felt immediately that the sweep of the living room should respond almost literally to the sweep of the view. My final design for the house had a curved outer wall that did just that.

Many other impressions, memories, and images become part of the brew that bubbles around in my head before I make my first sketch. Some ingredients are as seemingly frivolous as my wife's "quacker" earrings. When I was trying to describe to her how I'd come up with the basic idea for Wind Whistle, I jotted down a few notes: "dreams, cloud formations, English country cottages, Susan's quirky earrings,

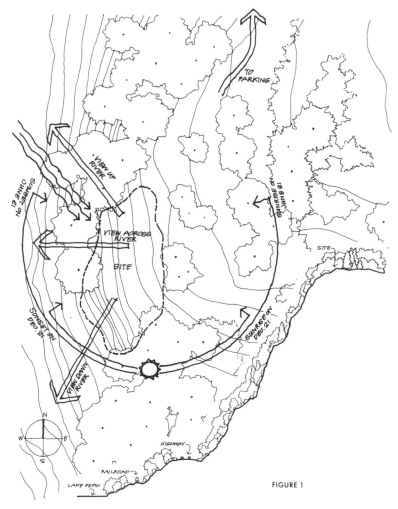

FIGURE 1

the quackers." She loves funny, often gaudy earrings in bright colors, especially those that have a touch of humor: plastic fortune cookies with an inscription inside, for example, or black cats. They sound dreadful, but I find them delightful, and she wears them with characteristic verve. Her "quackers" are particular favorites, a pair of yellow-and-blue wooden ducks, about 1½ inches long, that she bought in Covent Garden. The woman who made and sold them said, "Oh yes, you want the quackers." And that's how we refer to them. Those earrings symbolize to me part of Susan's spirit that I wanted to embody in Wind Whistle.

Of course, I do not work in an intellectual vacuum. No one does. All those who create do so from an unfathomable reservoir. Few, if any, of my designs over the years have been the direct result of one particular course of travel or study, but certainly the books I've read, the trips I've taken, and the buildings I've walked in and around have all influenced my ideas. I have mentioned many of these influences in Chapter 6, "Who's Holding the Pencil?"

During the years I've known her, Susan has often taught a course in creative writing, sometimes rather reluctantly. I've heard her say many times that she doesn't encourage her students to take writing courses at the expense of literature. "I'd rather have you read Chaucer, Shakespeare, Milton, Jane Austen, Dickens," she tells them. "What I can't teach you, but reading can, is a sense of rhythm, a feeling for words, an instinct for when a sentence sounds right." I feel the same way about architecture. Every experience with an interesting building— which might be a simple Provençal stone farmhouse or the New York Public Library or a Purcell, Feick & Elmslie Prairie Style house in Red Wing, Minnesota—enlarges my perceptions. Each may alter in some subtle, indefinable way how I approach my next design problem.

It isn't easy to say exactly where the idea comes from. It *is* easy to describe the "how" of how I get started. I sit down with my materials. I find that I'm ready to begin designing as soon as I have a pen or pencil and some paper with blank places on it. This confidence comes with much practice. Most architectural students at first do not know about how and where to get started; unless they are vigorously encouraged and directed, they often sit and stare at their boards for hour after hour.

When I first begin sketching, a rough and dreamy process that is more like thinking aloud, I use any scraps of paper that seem handy. (Susan justly complains about finding her grocery lists, memos to herself, opened letters, and even the telephone book covered with my scribbles whenever I begin a new project.) Later I'll work with a scale (an architect's ruler, which shows how to reduce measurements in scale, so each marking of ⅛, ¼, ½ inch, etc., equals a foot). I'll also soon move to a roll of yellow tracing paper, which architects call "bumwad," perhaps because it is the texture of old-fashioned English toilet paper and perhaps also because it gets wadded up and thrown away so often. Many, many design ideas do indeed go down the tube!

"Do you start with a floor plan, or with an external form?" Susan asked me, still hoping she might be able to trace the exact evolution of an architectural design. "Both," I said, to her quiet frustration. I do start with a floor plan, which arranges rooms and circulation into a reasonable relationship, but I always have an eye on architectural character.

In fact, almost anyone, with determination, a little observation and reading, and some practice, can develop a fairly good plan. Many people find a plan in a book or in one of the proliferating house magazines. They gerrymander the plan around to fit their own conditions, eliminating a room here, adding a closet there, moving a fireplace or wedging another bathroom next to the laundry room. Then they stick a roof on the plan (not always so easy), pick some exterior materials based on the "styles" they've seen, maybe add some half-timbering (Elizabethan), natural redwood siding (rustic), fancy gables (French Provincial), or columns and fake pediments (Colonial). Lots of their owners love these houses. But this is not the kind of house I design. I work for a harmonious and poetic whole.

Although my first drawings are freehand and sketchy, they are always to scale. I see no point in not being realistic at the very beginning. I start at a very small scale, usually $\frac{1}{16}$ inch equaling one foot. This small scale makes it easier to test out many plan arrangements, cross sections, elevations, and perspectives. As my scale grows larger, I begin making overlays of tracing paper so that I can change a design without redrawing the entire plan. Through overlay upon overlay, I can take an idea and develop it in a kind of natural evolution. Even when the last stage of a particular idea proves to be a dead end, I am glad I have tried it to the fullest extent possible.

I test out a number of alternative ideas to make sure that I've finally decided upon the best one possible. The first idea may turn out to be the final one, but I can discover this only by testing it against others. At this point I don't worry about how dumb or silly an idea might be. An architect has to explore many options, take some chances, and expand his or her range. (Still, at this stage, I don't like to have colleagues looking over my shoulder.)

I never share these early ideas with my client. I do not believe in showing clients a range of possibilities, like a smorgasbord, and letting them pick one. I believe that is an evasion of my own responsibility, the job for which I've been hired: to develop and recommend a specific design, with careful explanation for my choice. If my client hates it, I go back to the drawing board and try again.

Once I've settled on an idea I think may really work, I begin studying it in greater detail. I draw it out at a scale of ⅛ inch to one foot (twice the size of my earlier sketches). Now I'll begin having it modeled in cardboard as well. It is a time-consuming process, starting with a base that is true to the contours of the site. The first model is usually at ⅛ inch to one foot; walls are cut out and then the roof, and sometimes the roof is made to lift off, so we can see more directly what is inside. This is a rough model, mainly to show basic forms. For the client we make a more finished model, with windows and doors cut out, overhangs and other details added, and the site more fully articulated.

Clients get to take the finished models home, of course, for study and discussion, and I'm always pleased to see a couple walking out of my office, excited and talking together, model held carefully under the husband's or wife's arm. I sometimes suspect that the pleasure of creating models is a good key to the profession as a whole: for those of us who love it, it's just a heck of a lot of fun.

Until I've studied the three-dimensional aspects of my design in a model, I can't make a judgment on whether it is going to work. I also use many cross sections, drawings that cut through the house from top to bottom to reveal the nature of the interior spaces. I study these to check the proportions of the rooms and their relationships.

Designing a house is not steady progress. It is a halting flow, and what seems like an exciting breakthrough one night will look mediocre or inappropriate the next morning. Like other creative people, an architect can get stuck. I usually then go for a walk, take in a movie, lie awake at night for a while, and finally talk over my problem with a trusted colleague.

As my clients and I work together, I reassure them that the idea is a preliminary one. At this stage we can ask each other lots of questions. They can criticize the plan and suggest changes, but I also ask them to take some risks. If the idea I show them is quite different from what they had expected—and it often is—I ask them to consider it and then talk it over with me. In fact, I usually suggest that they don't give me their first impressions right away, unless they are very, very sure of them. I explain the drawings, give them the model, and set up a meeting later to talk it all over.

When my clients and I meet again, we discuss, compromise, and arrive at an understanding. Since I believe that the relationship between architect and client helps the architect arrive at the best final design, my design work and our meetings may continue for quite a while, for days or weeks. Sometimes we agree on a design concept almost immediately, and then I move into what architects call "design development," which simply means refinement and completion.

Recently an old friend who runs a large farming operation in western Minnesota asked me to draw up a plan for a covered platform, not far from his house, where he and his wife could enjoy a wonderful view of the Lac Qui Parle River, which runs through his land. We didn't discuss structure or forms. I eventually presented them with a model of a small one-room building, a kind of indoor/

outdoor gazebo, based partly on the shape of old-fashioned barns. It was a unique structure, unlike anything in their environment, and indeed unlike anything else I have ever designed, though it is neither shocking nor determinedly idiosyncratic. Susan, who speaks a little French, says it is a *jeu d'esprit*. I change the translation a bit and call it Gerry and Pat's "place of the spirit."

After studying the model, they told me, with the frankness of long friendship, that it looked "like an upside-down boat." But, open to its possibilities, they also responded to the model and soon decided that they liked it. We discussed, modified, and agreed. I continued with my design work, and when the building was complete, we all loved it. Folks from "town" are still somewhat skeptical.

I *want* to love every house I build. I need to be as satisfied with it as my clients are. Other kinds of artists can hide work they've done, perhaps early in their career or during a down time, and they don't have to show it to anybody they don't want to, even for a retrospective. But architects' mistakes are very visible, for a very long time. Since I've been in practice almost forty years, I've made a few myself. I still cringe a bit when I drive by a certain building in Minneapolis that didn't turn out as well as I'd hoped. Oh, I could explain its mediocrity away with lots of extenuating circumstances, but what good would that do? There the building stands, and I usually take a particular route to avoid seeing it.

So when I am settling on a design, testing and refining it, I have a lot at stake for myself as well as for my clients. I want the house to embody the values I care about: organic unity, pleasing form, and fitting relationship to its environment, as well as interior virtues of well-planned space and circulation, ample natural lighting, comfort, and convenience. Of course, I want the finished house to look great. I'm a little shy about calling a house I've designed a work of art, but if I'm lucky, and everything has gone right, that's what it should be.

I want the house to have its own character, yet to be something that is mine as well. One of the hardest tasks for an architect over the years is to avoid the passing clichés, the fads in style that change every few years. When an architect reads, travels, and observes, he or she can easily pick up certain ideas that are simply in the air, and those ideas can influence designs almost unconsciously. Sometimes that's fine; most of the time, such imitation leads to artificiality. Susan talks passionately about how she must be true to her own voice as a writer, and the same compulsion should drive an architect. I want to design a house I can proudly claim in five, ten, or twenty-five years.

Once a project enters the phase of design development, detail becomes very important. This is an exacting part of the process—choosing materials, locating windows, planning driveways and landscaping, making certain that everything fits together. I lay out the kitchen, design the fireplace, and locate bookshelves. I make furniture layouts to test the shape and size of the rooms, and if my clients have certain pieces already in mind, I test those for scale. As a measure of how much time all this takes, most architects allot only 15 percent of their fee for schematic design and 20 percent for design development.

When the design is complete, I sit down with structural and mechanical engineers and review the whole project. These specialists are not members of the architect's office, but every office has affiliation with one or more teams of engineers they like and trust. The engineers' knowledge is essential to design development. They'll tell me if my roof might sag, or if one wing of the house might get too cold, or if a six-zone heating and cooling system is too expensive. They'll also tell me what to do about it.

Now I am ready to prepare the working drawings and specifications, which some architects call the "contract documents." This is not as dull and rote a process as it sounds. Indeed, an architect must produce these finished drawings with the same high level of design consciousness that he or she used in the preceding stages. In a larger office, one or more architects besides the designer may have a hand in drawing; I enjoy doing them myself when I have the time.

Working drawings tell the builders in technical detail what is to be built. I try not to tell more than I know. Many construction details can and should be left to the individual artisans, who are expert in ways I am not. If I have designed a brick wall, for example, I will indicate its elevation, the color of the brick, the pattern and coursings, and how I want it to look. I will not try to tell the mason where to put his weep holes or how to make the wall moistureproof. (What architect doesn't know the story of rain that came right through a brick wall?) Although I indicate to the carpenters what kind of roof I want, I don't also instruct them how to apply the shingles.

The drawings include the broad outlines of construction: size of the structure, exterior and interior elevations, walls, door and window sizes, cabinet details, and the identification of all materials. They also show such details as railings, built-in tables, and other special features. Although some architects leave the placement of lighting to electrical engineers, I consider the lighting such an important element in design and in its effects that I design the lighting layouts and select the fixtures (in consultation with the client).

In our office, a set of drawings for an average house will consist of fifteen sheets, 24×36 inches. For Wind Whistle, a fairly small house, there were thirteen (see three of them in Figures 2, 3, and 4). These tracing-paper drawings are then run through a copying machine to produce several sets of blueprints, those familiar large blue pieces of paper that almost everyone recognizes as the professional signature of an architect. (They are actually blue lines on white paper.) A smart homeowner will keep a set of these blue-

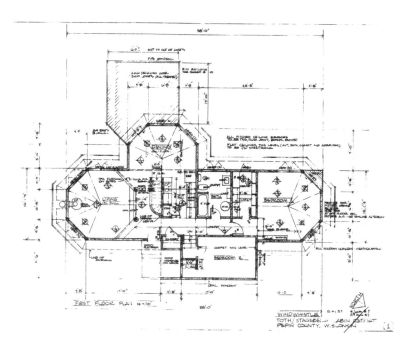

FIGURE 2

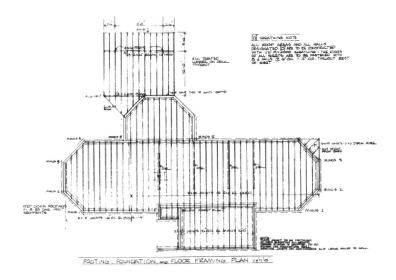

FIGURE 3

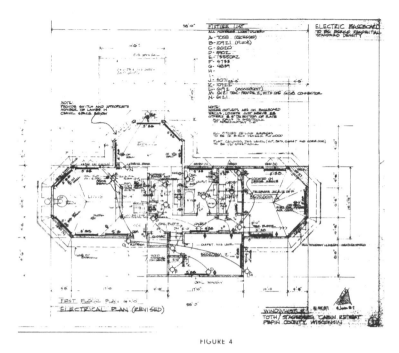

FIGURE 4

prints, rolled up and securely stashed in some unforgettable place, for a later day when he or she or another owner may want to make a repair or remodel or add to the house.

Accompanying the working drawings will be written specifications that elaborate on the standards of construction, the quality and types of materials, special equipment, and much other information. My usual set of "specs" averages thirty-five typewritten $8\frac{1}{2} \times 11$-inch sheets. (I've reproduced four of these—Appendix C.) Although they don't make particularly scintillating reading, they may help reassure you that your architect does more for his or her fee than just build a nice model. (For a very full discussion of the sort of specifications required to build a proper house, see Jim Locke's *The Well-Built House*.)

The first use of these contract documents—working drawings plus specifications—is for pricing. I usually give a half-dozen sets to each of three carefully selected builders and ask each to give me a lump-sum bid for construction of the house. (For other ways to handle this aspect of bidding, see Chapter 4, "What Will It All Cost?")

These documents ensure that each of the contractors and subcontractors (those who furnish lumber, provide the plumbing and heating, apply the wallboard, etc.) will be bidding on exactly the same data. One won't be planning to build a Ford while the other envisions a BMW. Once the builder, usually the low bidder, is chosen, these same contract documents become the basis for construction.

The design process officially ends when construction begins, although changes, selections, and new decisions continue to be made (as you'll see in Chapter 14, "The Construction Process"). Groundbreaking is an exciting event for both client and architect, and I encourage my clients to celebrate it. When I began an addition to my house upon Susan's and my marriage, we arranged a short ceremony, with the builder and two close friends. Everyone spoke briefly about hopes for this new beginning, and we all dug a token shovelful of dirt. Then we went inside for coffee and rolls and let the excavator begin the real work.

When construction began on Wind Whistle, Susan and I were out of the country, but we often imagined and anticipated what was happening several thousand miles away. A few hours after we got home, we ignored jet lag and rushed down to the site. There wasn't much more to admire than a large hole in the ground, but as we looked at the foundation, we could envision the house that would eventually take shape. The design process had worked its magic, and Wind Whistle had already begun to live.

THE LIVING ROOM: HEART OF THE HOUSE

Living rooms have always been special places. The very phrase suggests that *this* is the place where everything happens. The first living room was probably some kind of cave. Vast and uncomfortable as they look to us today, ancient baronial halls were living rooms, where nobles met their retainers, feasted, and warmed themselves before a huge fire. The New England "parlor," containing a family's best furniture and china, was a sort of living room, too, even if it was used mainly for formal occasions.

In Dawson, the Minnesota small town where I grew up, living rooms, set apart in use and in atmosphere from the rest of the house, traced their ancestry to parlors. Most household activities took place in the kitchen, often around a large round table. Our living room served only for Sundays or visits by the preacher, teacher, or out-of-town relatives. Since our house was small, so was our living room, but it always held our most prized possessions: a leather sofa and armchair, a handsome console radio, hand-crocheted doilies, and a few china vases.

Not long ago, a proud owner of a new house in Minneapolis showed me through his large and elegant rooms. The family room, which looked well used, was "just for us," and the living room, he said, was "for entertaining." For most of us, however, the living room has to combine both entertaining and family-room functions. It has become the heart of the house, a room we use every day. Kitchen, dining area, bathrooms, bedrooms, studies are all important, and a good architect does not give them less attention, either in functional or in aesthetic terms. But if a house is well designed, rooms have an appropriate hierarchy, and for most clients, the living room is always at the top.

When, through renovation, addition, or new construction, a family has a chance to create a living room from the ground up, the space can and should reflect their ideas of who they are and of what they do. The clients must describe how they will use their living room. Do they like to entertain? If so, do they often invite large groups of people? (An architect must provide enough space for at least some of them to sit down while others mill around comfortably.) Do they see themselves in a cozy space or in a formal one? Is the living room a place where they will watch television? Listen to music? Play music? Will the living room combine with a dining room for eating space? Do they own books, and is this the room in which the books belong? How close should the kitchen be, and how should it relate to the living room? Do they have a large dog? An aquarium?

As always, the size of the living room will be determined not only by the "program" (the set of needs the room must meet) but by the budget. Sometimes clients can delegate some of these "living-room functions" to another room, perhaps a family room or a study or a bedroom. Difficult choices may have to be made: if the television and stereo are both in the living room, where will someone sit to read?

As I ask these questions, I try not to impose my own answers. We all live differently, and what works for me might not work for others. In Susan's and my house in Minneapolis, our living room is quite small. I initially designed it just for myself, and when we married, our remodeling funds went into a new bedroom, much larger, more dramatic, and more compartmentalized than the living room. The bedroom has shelves lined with many of Susan's books, a cushioned window seat, and a raised nook with fireplace and easy chairs. We read here, rather than in the living room, and sometimes visit with a friend near the fireplace.

At Wind Whistle, our living room is quite different. There it is the center of family activity, a snug refuge where we enjoy the fireplace eight months of the year, gaze through the most windows at the Mississippi below, read, and listen to music. An overlay drawing of Wind

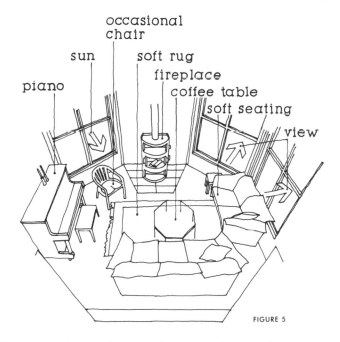

FIGURE 5

Whistle (Figure 5) shows the requirements I consider essential for a living room: ample sunlight; soft seating suitable for lounging; an occasional chair for additional guests; a table to hold books, magazines, drinks; a music center, here with piano and radio/cassette player; a fireplace; and a soft rug. I recommend a similar list to my clients, although some prefer variations—a strategically placed television set, for example.

As a glance at a color illustration of the living room at Wind Whistle reveals, this octagonal room is not large, only about fifteen feet across, but it has a spacious feeling. Seating is planned to gather people around the fireplace, facing each other, but also taking in the view of Lake Pepin to the right. The special qualities of the room derive from a high ceiling, a dormer window with sky view, a change in levels via a two-step platform, and a lighthearted color scheme.

When a designer begins to plan a living room for a client, he or she takes the list of the client's needs and wishes and adds (I hope) talent and imagination. Over the years I've found certain rules that help create a living room that is both functional and pleasant.

First, an architect must create the proper traffic-circulation system for a house: one that allows clear and easy access to the living room, but that does *not* require everyone to pass through the living room in order to get to another room. A child dragging a toy truck should not have to mark a path on the living-room carpet in order to reach the family room. A teenager grabbing a snack in the kitchen doesn't want to pad past all her parents' guests in order to reach her bedroom. Someone cooking dinner for friends would rather not have to stroll past them, with a few muttered words of explanation, in order to get to the bathroom. The living room should not serve as Grand Central Station for the house.

A good designer should provide the living room with the best possible view. You may be lucky enough to look out over marsh or countryside or city lake, or you may have a view over your own small private yard with shrubs and flowers. A designer can even create a view. From our bedroom in our remodeled Minneapolis house, I framed a view of a scraggly apple tree through a strategically placed window. When we look out, we see branches against the sky in a changing seasonal design, and we feel as if we are living among treetops—instead of on a narrow city lot with a stamp-size backyard. A window can also frame a view of angled rooftops so that it seems like a carefully composed abstract painting. We are fond of a certain room in a small and somewhat creaky New York hotel whose back windows give fascinating views onto the neighboring rooftops, terraces, and even penthouses. Almost any living room can be oriented to at least one attractive view.

While the architect is thinking about views, he or she will also consider available natural light. A living room that is dark all day is depressing. If tall buildings or trees block the sun except at certain times and in certain directions, an architect will plan to maximize those conditions. Most regions of the United States have some sunshine year-round, and some of that sun belongs in the living room.

Although I feel strongly about the psychological and aesthetic advantages of natural light, I use it judiciously. Some people think it would be delightful to live in a glass house. They rhapsodize about "the feeling of being outdoors all the time" or "living close to nature" or "watching the weather." In most climates, too much glass or poorly located glass will prove to be a mistake. Even if the client doesn't care about the cost of heating, and even if the glass is double- or triple-glazed, many of us feel chilled when exposed for any length of time to a cold glass wall. Drafts are also a problem, no matter how effectively the room is sealed, because hot air rises and cooler air takes its place, causing chilly breezes.

Excessive use of glass is also a problem during hot weather. Think of how your car feels after it has been parked for an hour in summer sunshine. Of course, heavy drapes can cut heat and glare, but who wants to spend time in a room in which the drapes are constantly drawn? We gave up living in caves for good reasons. The technology of glass is fast-moving, and new products are now being developed that permit higher efficiency, certain colorations, and restricted intake of light rays. These products are often quite expensive, however, and I do not specify them for most of the houses I design. So although I use glass generously, striving for an effect of airiness and openness, I thoroughly consider its size and placement.

An architect must also plan glass carefully in a house that is close to other houses. It must be limited, strategically positioned, and/or baffled, for the windows that face neighbors directly. (Baffles are like vertical blinds, only placed outside the house; they are walls or fins that allow direct but not sideways vision.) No one except an exhibitionist wants to live in a fishbowl, and a glass tank does not make a warm and welcoming living room.

Together with light, I consider furniture placement in the first stages of living-room design. If someone is lying down on the sofa, what happens to the view? If someone is sitting in an easy chair, can he or she see the television? Is the television positioned to avoid glare from a window? Can a guest sitting in the occasional chair easily reach a coffee table? Nothing is more annoying than trying to carry on a conversation in a crowded room while searching for a place to set down a drink.

As I consider furniture placement, I often focus on the fireplace, a favorite feature of temperate-zone living rooms. Of all the fixtures in a room, the fireplace is the most challenging to design. I'm often surprised to find in otherwise well-planned houses how difficult it is to sit around a fireplace in a natural way. The seating arrangement must be carefully planned, because people *do* want to sit, rather than stand in front of the flames, at a comfortable distance. Although I've seen advertisements (for everything from whiskey to life insurance) that show a distinguished gentleman, one hand in his smoking jacket, casually leaning against a mantel over a glowing fire, I'll bet he jumped away from the heat the moment he heard the photographer's click.

In most climates (even here in Minnesota!), a fireplace is idle for many months of the year. A designer needs to make sure the empty hearth is not an eyesore during the warm season. If a fireplace is a pleasing sculptural object, it will attract admiring attention on its own —but without dominating the room. On a recent trip to England, when Susan and I visited Standen, a delightful house designed in the 1890s by Philip Webb and furnished with William Morris designs, I took several pictures of the different fireplaces—all without fires, for it was a warm and sunny summer day. Their white-painted mantels and surrounding wainscoting were ornamented yet unobtrusive, restrained in feeling but vintage artifacts of the spirited Arts and Crafts movement. A contemporary fireplace can have that kind of design distinction too.

In both my current house in Minneapolis and at Wind Whistle, I have chosen to forgo fireplaces in favor of freestanding wood-burning stoves. Especially at Wind Whistle, a stove can be a critical source of heat during a possible power outage in midwinter. Stoves are more efficient than fireplaces, since the entire heat-emanating body remains in the room. Although I did not design either stove, I looked long and hard in catalogs, magazines, and showrooms for the right one for each space. Some wood-burning stoves look so goofy that they skew the appearance of the whole living room. The black Danish stove at Wind Whistle is simple and striking, an accent that adds to the room in summer as well as winter.

A designer often has to take into account the furniture his or her clients already own and plan to use. One recent client, for example, had painstakingly acquired many large Victorian pieces intended for the living room. The towering breakfront and ponderous clawfooted sofa dictated a living room of ample proportions. Occasionally an architect encounters furniture he or she just cannot stand, and this presents a tricky situation. Without insulting a valued client's taste, I usually try to suggest the drawbacks of, say, a fake wrought-iron coffee table with spindly legs and overdone curlicues in a sleek modern room with a light oak floor. Sometimes it works, sometimes not. A client's interior decorator may help, exerting a firm authority that would seem tyrannical in an architect. When my clients rely on only my advice for furniture style and placement, however, I try to find the right time to tell them what I think. Sometimes the time is never right; I tell them anyway.

An architect also needs information about special collections requiring display or storage in the living room. When Susan and I married, she warned me that she wouldn't move unless she could bring all her books—a collection she'd been amassing since childhood. So I knew that our addition and remodeling would have to include many running feet of bookshelves. Most of them are in our bedroom and study, but I did add some shelves in the living room, as well as space for records and piano music. Some clients have paintings requiring large wall areas, and others might want a niche for plants or for a display of Depression glass.

A memorable living room depends on one last factor—creativity, which is almost impossible to describe. In Chapter 7, "The Design Process," I talked about how I arrive at a design, and I drew a spiral that finally zeros in on an idea, at a center which I labeled "ZOW!" The "zow" factor is what finally makes a living room a very special place that not only fills your needs but delights you. A living room with the "zow" factor is not just a soaring ceiling, or color-stained paneling, or unusual bookcases, but a unified concept. Imagination comes easily to many people, and we daydream all the time, but transforming those ideas into an integrated design is *not* so easy. Some people are skilled enough to do this themselves, and others decide to use the services of one or more design professionals. That is my business, and if I do it right, both my clients and I will end up toasting each other in a light-filled, comfortable, well-planned, and even stunning living room.

THE OTHER IMPORTANT ROOMS

No one except the tenant of a one-room apartment lives in a living room all the time. The other rooms in a house—those for eating, sleeping, bathing, storing—are also important, and a thoughtful architect will give them meticulous attention. From the entry to the basement, each area has its own requirements and its own possibilities for distinction.

Although it is usually not a separate room, the entry to a house is both an introduction and a farewell, and it deserves a bit of fanfare. From the exterior, the entry should be marked not only by a walk or by landscaping, but also by an architectural feature. Even in a house where the front door is dead center in the facade, an appropriately distinguished entry clearly announces "Welcome." The entry might be set into a recess, crowned with a pediment, or, in period houses or in postmodern whimsies, framed by columns. An overhang will not only mark an entry but provide shelter when the owner is juggling keys and groceries in a rainstorm.

Often an entry includes a "stoop," an unappealing word that makes me think of someone with a bent back trying to squeeze into an oversmall door (and that is actually descended from the Dutch *stoep*, meaning "step"). The stoop is a platform just outside the front door, something approached by a few steps, if the door is not at ground level. Since it gets heavy wear, the material for the stoop should be durable, maybe brick or stone (my favorite choices) or concrete (which is cheaper).

Concrete *can* be treated in a variety of ways to enhance it visually. An architect can select the small stones used for the aggregate that makes up concrete, and then these stones can be ground down or exposed. I sometimes use marble chips, for example, or a color of limestone that my client likes. Inserts of wood or metal can also give a pattern to the concrete.

Crossing the threshold, a visitor has a first impression of the house, its character, and the kind of people who live in it. So the entryway must also make a statement. It need not be large; in fact, it should be sized in proportion to the rest of the house. What looks more pretentious, for example, than a towering marble-floored entry hall that leads into a tiny apartment? Even a small area, however, can have some spatial distinction, perhaps added height or an unusual shape or a high window that throws light onto the entry below. In a traditional Colonial house, the entry usually faces a stairway rising to the second floor; this immediate view gives the entry a feeling of height. In my own Minneapolis house, our small entry occupies the full height of the house, with a railing above on the end of the second-floor hall, so someone standing upstairs can peer down to see who is knocking at the front door.

The function of an entry is not only to introduce a visitor into the house but also to assist in a physical transition from outdoors to indoors. So an entry floor has to handle wet shoes and boots, and a coat closet must be placed conveniently nearby. To solve the messy aspects of this transition, some houses include a "mud room" in addition to the entry. "Mud room" is something of a misnomer, since after the mess of house construction is over, no one (at least in a city with sidewalks) should have to tramp through mud to get to the front door. But, like a pantry off a kitchen, a mud room off an entry is a useful storage and behind-the-scenes dumping place.

Every house has a dumping place, whether owners acknowledge it or not. This is where, upon entering, everyone drops keys or heaps the mail or stashes books, bundles, gloves, and other paraphernalia. I don't like the look of clutter, so I think the "dumping place" should be behind doors, rather than on a visible piece of furniture. Since we don't have a mud room in our Minneapolis house, I have to admit that we tend to toss not our boots, but at least our hats and keys on the dining-room table. Better that, I tell myself, than a heaped-up small table in our entry.

Once past the entry, an architect confronts other and larger rooms about which the clients usually have strong feelings. Whoever does the family cooking, for example, will probably have already developed a wish list for the new kitchen. So many people want an ideal kitchen that how-to pamphlets, magazines, and entire books have been developed to meet the market, along the line of *Dream Kitchens* or *Guide to a Great Kitchen*. Many of my clients bring well-thumbed copies of such magazines or books to our first conference. Although these beautifully illustrated volumes can be fun to look at, and some guides give useful information, such as the standard sizes of refrigerators and stoves or the options in sinks, most of the pictured dream kitchens are far grander and more expensive than most of my clients want or can afford, or they are just not appropriate for a variety of other reasons.

Sometimes a client asks about consulting a specialty firm that does nothing but plan kitchens. Such firms are undoubtedly valuable for people building a house or renovating a kitchen without an architect. They advertise locally, again with gleaming high-tech pictures, and often sell cabinets and other fixtures to make their necessary profit. Although I never discourage a client from exploring alternatives, I have never felt the need of "specialists" in planning a kitchen. Architects not only integrate the kitchen with the other rooms of the house, but they also know sources for kitchen cabinets that are every bit as attractive and functional as the showroom models and are often less expensive.

Since I like to cook myself, I know that many people spend more working hours in the kitchen than in any other room, and they want a design that offers the modern conveniences and a pleasant and cheery environment as well. The kitchen should be wisely located, not too far from the front door or on another level; the cook should not have to make a mad dash to answer the doorbell. Certain basics of room design apply to the kitchen as much as to other rooms: good light, sunshine at some time of the day, access to a view. Most cooks want to look at something other than a cabinet when they are washing, scrubbing, peeling, and chopping.

Although the window over the sink in our Minneapolis house looks onto our private backyard, at Wind Whistle I had to locate the kitchen with a side view in order to give the dining area a prime perspective over the river. We spend less time cooking at our vacation house but we linger over our meals longer, so my compromise made sense.

Designing a functional kitchen is not difficult, and most of my clients already know some of the fundamentals, such as making sure the stove, sink, and refrigerator form a reasonably compact triangle. (Even in a large kitchen designed to hold lots of kibitzing guests, a cook has to be able to move a pot of boiling pasta quickly from stove to sink.) This triangle has many successful variations. The clients will then need to decide on the number and kind of appliances: a stove with an oven, or range top and built-in ovens? Microwave? Dishwasher? Trash compactor? Grill? Extra sink? Each additional appliance, of course, requires additional space.

The size of a kitchen depends not only on the owner's budget and allocation of funds but on life-styles. Some people want to eat and entertain in the kitchen, and others simply want an efficient and compact space where they plan to spend as little time as possible. Within that wide range of size, a kitchen has certain practical minimums and maximums. For a normal family house, the minimum counter space, including appliances, I have found acceptable is about twenty-two linear feet, and many families want more. In our Minneapolis house, originally designed just for myself, we have less, and Susan and I come close to sharp words when all kinds of things appear on our kitchen counters, from napkin holders to Cuisinart to memos to clipped recipes. If I were designing the kitchen all over again, knowing she'd be living with me, I'm sure I'd add an extra mile.

Eating space in a kitchen is also a matter of user preference. I differ from most of my clients, who usually want a small eating area, formerly called a "dinette" or "breakfast nook." Since I care a lot about my environment when I eat, I prefer to have one dining space in my house, located in the best environment possible, with good light, height, and views. I use dining furniture that can serve both for everyday and for special dinners. (Susan accuses me, with some justice, of refusing to stop at any restaurant that is dark or low-ceilinged or has plastic trees.) I don't want to grab a quick bite at a small table in the kitchen. I'd rather sit at a spacious dining table and look out the window—which is the way we eat both at our Minneapolis home and at Wind Whistle. Why perch on a stool as if at a diner?

Once the size and configuration of the kitchen is decided, my clients and I need to decide about cabinets. Materials and finishes must be durable; a kitchen gets a lot of wear and can show it. I prefer doors, drawer fronts, and cabinet ends—the parts everyone sees—in some variety of wood, often solid boards, and often oak. Sometimes these visible parts are plywood with veneer and occasionally plastic laminate. All these alternatives are equally sturdy, and they do not vary much in cost. A choice is a matter of visual preference. Because cabinets look best stopped by a ceiling rather than hanging in midair, I usually plan an eight- or nine-foot ceiling, not higher, for the kitchen. (Anyone wanting extra storage is probably better off with an adjoining pantry or pantry-type closet rather than with storage areas that are too high to reach. I often specify a walk-in pantry and always at least a pantry closet that is conveniently located).

If a client has some special cabinet features in mind—revolving turntables, wine rack, drop-down ironing board—I usually ask the client to meet with the cabinetmaker and work out details. Since I have estimated a budget for cabinets, the clients and cabinetmaker work within this dollar amount, or if the owners ask for more than the budget has allowed, they order more with the knowledge that it will be an additional cost.

Besides cabinets, the client needs to select countertop material and color. As I've mentioned, most of my kitchens use plastic laminate, the generic term for the material known popularly by one of its brand names, Formica. "Butcher-block" wood tops look great at first, but after a few knife slashes, pizza stains, and water marks, they discolor badly. Solid vinyl is fairly expensive, and tile, like marble, is hard and noisy. An irritated teenager stacking dishes on a tile countertop can express a lot of frustration quite effectively, not to mention what happens when he or she "accidentally" flips over a crystal goblet. So most of my clients choose plastic laminate, which now comes in many colors. At Wind Whistle, the apple-green countertop carries out the fresh and lively greens elsewhere in the house.

One of the hardest decisions to make is the choice of floor material. None is perfect. Vinyl works and wears well, but I'm afraid I think it looks rather, well, commercial, or even cheap. Tile is hard and shatters dropped glassware (as it does on a countertop), and it can be very tricky to keep clean. Susan and I once stayed in a friend's Arizona vacation house, and we spent a lot of time sweeping and mopping so no one would find our crumbs on the shiny white tile floor of the kitchen. A stone floor has some of the same problems of hardness and upkeep;

any shiny or polished surface will show soil. But some clients are willing to sacrifice cleaning time for the undeniable good looks of stone. In one house I've just designed, the Bavarian limestone floor is carried throughout the entry, corridors, and fireplace area. It is a striking ensemble, and the owners are happy with it.

Because kitchens are now more open than they used to be, kitchen flooring will affect the whole feeling of the house. Often it continues most naturally from the dining area, rather than stopping abruptly at a hypothetical line. Lately I have favored hardwood with a polyurethane finish for the dining and kitchen floors. It looks warm yet functional, and short-term maintenance is easy. Over a number of years, however, most hardwood floors can't really resist a steady onslaught of spills and splashes and the crisscross patterns of heavy traffic without refinishing. A good Oriental rug—one that costs a few hundred dollars, not a museum-quality rug—placed in front of the sink is almost impervious to wear, hides stains, softens the hard floor, and adds intriguing color and pattern to the design scheme. Best of all, it greatly reduces maintenance of the hardwood floor.

Even if a house is designed with an eating area in the kitchen, most people want a larger and more formal dining space elsewhere. Few if any clients ask for a dining *room*, closed off by doors from the rest of the house, perhaps partly because most houses I design are not extremely large or elaborate structures. Since my clients lead servantless, casual lives, they want their activities integrated, rather than sharply defined, in the design of their houses.

Most dining areas, for obvious reasons of convenience, need to be close to the kitchen. Because nobody wants to dawdle over dessert while staring at a pile of dirty dishes, I am careful to provide a shield of some kind between the two spaces. The visual barrier might be as simple as a ledge or a countertop with a high back.

A dining area should be a space so special that it makes every meal an occasion. Every one I have ever designed has had some kind of visual pleasure connected with it — perhaps a view, or height, or an unusual shape. This special quality doesn't depend upon size. Our dining area in Minneapolis, which I designed when I was single, is only about 200 square feet, but it rises two stories (the full height of the house), has a view across the living room toward a lake, and has natural lighting from the south. At Wind Whistle, the dining area opens to the living room, rises as high, and looks downriver at a magnificent view. If a dining area has such compelling attractions, it soon becomes one of the favorite spots in the house. Ours has become a gathering place for playing cards, writing letters, drawing plans, sorting mail, laying out pictures, and reading the newspapers.

Early in the design process, I ask what kind of dining table the client plans to use, not for style as much as for size, since I draw onto the plan a table that will help determine the size and shape of the room. I allow enough room for the chairs to be pulled back for casual seating. If the room is small, the chairs must be carefully selected to fit comfortably. I usually also design a wall-hung buffet, unless the client already has a freestanding piece of furniture that he or she deems essential. The buffet, with a cabinet below, will be the right height for serving food buffet-style, and it will stop short of the floor by about a foot. Cabinets that sink all the way to the floor in a dining room may appear to provide more storage, but the extra space is often inaccessible. You may end up crawling on hands and knees behind the chairs of your guests to get an extra napkin.

Besides kitchens, many clients have strong feelings about what they want in their bedrooms—at least in the "master" bedroom, if not in the kids' rooms and in guest bedrooms. The size of a bedroom can vary enormously. Not long ago houses were routinely described as a "two-bedroom house" or a "three-bedroom house" in order to indicate the size and cost of the house as a whole. But now some owners want to squeeze four or five bedrooms into a space that another client might divide into only two bedrooms. A two-bedroom house might be much fancier than a four-bedroom one.

The master bedroom—where the owners plan to sleep—usually is larger and has more amenities than the other bedrooms. Many of my clients want their own bathroom, at least one walk-in closet, and perhaps a sitting area. When I built an addition to my Minneapolis house at the time I married Susan, I asked her what kind of bedroom she had always wanted. With a sneaky reminder to me that she was surrendering forever a never-indulged love of old Victorian houses, she asked for a window seat and a fireplace. We had space for both. In one recently finished house, my clients asked for and got a master bedroom that included a fireplace, built-in television, walk-in closets, a shower room, a w.c., a Jacuzzi tub in its own alcove, a balcony overlooking a lake, and an adjacent roof deck. A bedroom can expand almost infinitely—if a client has an expansive budget.

All bedrooms deserve good light and some visual interest, usually achieved by an out-of-the-ordinary room shape (not just a bland rectangle) and/or varying ceiling height. If I can plan for someone lying in bed to have a pleasant view outside, so much the better, but if there is just one "best" view, I give it to the living/dining area. Susan wants to watch sky and trees as she falls asleep, and both in Minneapolis and at Wind Whistle, our bedrooms are designed to make her feel she is outdoors. Besides windows that open onto trees, one has a window high in the ceiling and the other a skylight. Skylights are a splendid way to make a bedroom feel removed from the ordinary, although too large a skylight or too many may make it difficult to darken the room properly.

A bedroom really needs only a bed, of course. And it needs privacy. I baffle sound by filling the walls and floor of the master bedroom with insulation first; if the budget allows, I do the same for the other bedrooms and bathrooms. The bedroom also needs visual privacy. When an inquisitive child or blundering guest opens the door, the bed should not be in the line of sight. The door, it almost goes without saying, must have a lock. I locate the bed on drawings in order to plan the sightlines accordingly. I also want to be sure the room is large enough and has the right shape to accommodate the bed or beds my clients want.

Most of my clients ask for good bedside reading lights. In my own houses, I provide small built-in shelves next to the beds to hold telephone, books, a drinking glass, and clamp-on swivel lamps, which swing handily around to shield the light from the other bed. Some people want to watch television from bed, so I may have to figure the right angles for viewing. I also make room for at least one chair in the bedroom, not necessarily for bedside guests, but for changing shoes or dropping a bathrobe or towel, or piling stacks of books.

If a house has several bedrooms, and it usually does, I encourage my clients to consider locating them on more than one level. A separate level or "floor" for children gives parents much more privacy in a brief retreat from their twenty-four-hour-a-day job. If the children are very small, an electronic monitor can relay every sound from a room on a separate level into the parents' room. But as children grow older, parents don't *want* to hear all those sounds! Then that distance can be a godsend.

In addition to their bedroom, many people have romantic dreams about a room whose function is quite basic—the bathroom. Just like kitchens, bathrooms have inspired an astonishing amount of illustrated fantasy in magazine articles and individual how-to books. I've never thought of bathrooms as the realm of romance in our culture, but some people evidently do. Although few newlyweds I've known have spent their honeymoons in the bathroom, honeymoon resort advertisements traditionally feature a huge bathroom, with a Jacuzzi or a pool-size heart-shaped tub. Similar merchandising techniques have provoked developers to include in their model homes glitzy bathrooms with gilded faucets and marbleized sunken tubs.

If someone wants a jazzy bathroom, I can design one, but most of my clients, fortunately, share my opinion that the bathroom is a practical necessity, not a showplace. As any reader can probably tell by now, I like my architecture plain but handsome. A room should simply do what it is supposed to do, with grace, charm, and style. A bathroom should be large enough for its functions, should contain the right combination of fixtures, and should be attractive and easy to clean. Everyone has different ideas about fixtures, and they are not always so easy to discuss. Sometimes an architect has to press rather delicately to make sure clients know and get what they're asking for. Susan berated me for ordering a bidet for Wind Whistle that didn't have an upward spray, which she graphically later explained was part of its raison d'être.

Like all rooms, a bathroom should have natural light and adequate ventilation. A bathroom without a window has an especially claustrophobic feeling. Once in London the only overnight space we could find quickly was in an older hotel, recommended and expensive, but limiting us to a room without bath. The bathrooms and separate toilets were down the hall. The toilet cubicle was just big enough for the fixture, it had no window, and its walls were unaccountably painted black. That dark and smelly little closet remains in my mind as a warning of the worst kind of bathroom.

For most people, closets and/or storage rooms are another essential. I recently studied with interest a news story about a prototype town house that could be built, with very small rooms and "no frills," for $62,000. It was a simple shell that had, among other exclusions, no closets. An owner could add freestanding wardrobes, chests of drawers, bookcases, and other storage devices, but every one of those items would eat up precious floor space. All my clients are passionate about storage space, and a well-designed house will include plenty of it.

Walk-in closets and storage rooms need to be dry, they should hold built-in shelving, and they need to be well lighted, with a window if possible. These guidelines exclude rooms in basements, unless they have been carefully constructed and insulated to prevent moisture and dampness. When stuff is hidden in closets, everyone forgets it. If it is stored on shelves in a walk-in room, people can often eventually recognize that it is redundant, no longer usable, or hopelessly outdated—and out it goes. Susan tends to stash and hoard, as she shamelessly admits. One evening when, not yet engaged, we were talking about the future, I looked around her house and assessed its accumulation of vases, mobiles, plants and, well, *stuff.* "If we ever get married, I'm going to rent you a Dumpster," I helpfully volunteered. Susan looked at me coldly and said, "*If* I ever get married again, which isn't likely, I am only going to marry a man who will promise to rent me a U-Haul." Life with Susan has made me even more aware of the need for shelves and storage.

Another kind of room almost everyone wants is a laundry. Once located in a basement—the safest place to wring out sopping clothes and suffer the occasional washer overflow without disaster—a laundry today is usually located near the kitchen or even the bedroom, both for convenience and for a pleasanter environment. Although some money is saved by placing plumbing (kitchen, bath, laundry) in horizontal and vertical proximity, the saving is not enough to justify planning the design around the plumbing. Modern appliances, properly installed, are fairly reliable. But accidents do happen, and so the laundry must have a drain and a water-resistant flooring, such as vinyl or ceramic tile.

The laundry should be well lit, of course, and I usually specify a fluorescent fixture, even two, although I never use such a blatantly utilitarian light in other rooms. The room or area should be large enough to hold an ironing board, as well as washer and dryer, probably a table or countertop for sorting clothes, and sometimes linen storage space. Since the laundry is a much-visited room, it should not be designed as a second-rate space, with exposed pipes and dangling cables. I try for the qualities of finish that I use in the rest of the house. The same magazines and books that describe glamorous kitchens and bathrooms often include some suggestions about laundry rooms, and I am happy to add whatever amenities my clients want. In our own house, the laundry room, located on a lower level that Susan stubbornly calls "the basement," even though it is nothing of the kind, also holds the freezer, shelves for stockpiled groceries, tools, unused flowerpots, the Christmas-tree stand, a picnic basket—well, you get the idea.

Most new houses do have basements. If unfinished, they are relatively cheap. In colder climates, since the house has to be placed on a foundation that goes well below the frost line anyway (moisture in the ground causes expansion during freezing, and a moving foundation would mean, at the very least, cracked walls), a basement seems almost inevitable. Basements do provide a place for mechanical equipment (furnace, hot-water heater, etc.). Some homeowners like to "finish" a basement into a space that used to be called a "rec room" and now is sometimes a play room or a party room, complete with wet bar. Although I'm supposed to be an unbiased interpreter of my clients' dream, I have a hard time hiding my aversion to fancily finished basements, especially as adult party rooms. Attending a social gathering held in a basement, no matter how cleverly disguised, tends to dampen my party mood. I think many children probably feel the same way. In theory, children should rush to a basement playroom with their friends and toys, but in practice, they often prefer to be upstairs near a sunny window. Even the family cat doesn't usually like being shut up in the basement. Too often homeowners invest too much money in a basement room that ends up merely as a graveyard for broken toys or card tables.

One extra I do get enthusiastic about is a sauna. Perhaps because most of my recent houses have been built in Minnesota, they all have included saunas, which are marvelously revitalizing when your bones know it's cold outside. Unless the below-ground space is a walkout, the sauna should never be located in a basement. After a sauna, you should be able to step almost directly outside, not necessarily to roll in the snow, but to enjoy a brisk cooling off as part of the sauna process. (Susan, who is tentative about saunas, tends to open the outside door, shiver a few times, and rush back into the heat. Since I've got more Scandinavian blood, I hang out a bit longer to show off.) At Wind Whistle, our sauna is on the level of the roof deck, and dashing outdoors in February, with a twenty-mile wind blowing off the lake, is a brisk experience indeed.

I size the sauna for just a few people, perhaps up to four. Mostly one or two will use the sauna on a regular basis, and a smaller sauna means not only less time and energy to heat up the room but also a cozier experience. A sauna should have a window. (Some people find a closed sauna a little claustrophobic.) At Wind Whistle, we look out a small window on twenty downstream miles of river.

Besides these basics, an architect can add all kinds of other rooms—again, as always, if budget and dreams are in synch. Library, study, music room, workshop, sewing room, greenhouse, potting shed—I've been asked for all these and more. But perhaps the most frequent request is for usable outdoor space. My clients love the idea of being able to step outside to a deck, balcony, porch, or patio. Every house I've ever designed has had at least one of these "outdoor rooms."

I am particularly fond of roof decks, perhaps because I often design houses with at least partially flat roofs. Years ago, when I was an architectural student, José Sert spoke eloquently about how architects did not make enough use of flat roofs as "found" living spaces. These roof decks can offer relatively bug-free environments, as well as views, breezes, and privacy. Although our Minneapolis house is on a busy city street, our roof deck is so protected by tree branches in the summer that we feel utterly removed from passing traffic. The top deck at Wind Whistle, small as it is, gives us the best perspective of the river below. Since Wind Whistle combines pitched roofs with flat, we also have an intriguing view of the detached roof shapes of the rest of the house.

I've already pointed out the erroneous assumption that flat roofs always cause more trouble than sloped roofs, but a flat roof covered with boards and then used as a walking surface is more vulnerable to leaks unless it is built properly with the correct materials. Both architect and builder have to do their homework in order to build a trouble-free roof deck. If neither has ever built a roof deck before, they will need to proceed with caution, because their laboratory is the client's home.

As part of a plan for a roof deck, an architect should provide planting areas and freestanding flowerboxes. Though planters can be simple and fairly inexpensive, they should be attractive. Our own roof deck in Minneapolis has rectangular redwood boxes. Once filled with dirt, such boxes are so heavy that they are immovable, so the client and architect should discuss sun and shade conditions before deciding where to place them.

Other outdoor spaces can include a patio, which is an outdoor surface that sits directly on the ground, with a hard floor usually of stone, brick, or concrete; balconies, much smaller than a deck, and usually a projection or cantilever from the house; and porches, covered and perhaps screened or partially enclosed. Dozens of permutations of these spaces are possible. At our Minneapolis home, we have a roof deck that includes a small screened gazebo. At Wind Whistle, we have a deck constructed on the bluff side, a small bedroom balcony, and a small roof deck. Like most homeowners, we love all these outdoor "rooms."

In our Midwestern climate, I prefer the floor surface for decks, balconies, and porches to be wood boards, spaced slightly apart to allow good water drainage. Wood is available and not too expensive, and it has a "soft" look and feel to it. It also dries quickly after rain or snow. I usually specify redwood or fir planks specially treated to reduce rot.

One detail that needs a designer's attention for any deck more than a foot from the ground, any balcony, or any porch is the railing. (A railing is mandated not only for safety but usually by building-code requirements.) The railing can have a surprising visual impact as well as a practical one, so it can't just be slapped together. It should feel absolutely sturdy. Nothing is more unsettling than leaning against a balcony railing high above the ground and feeling it "give," even a little. Frequently the railing tends to obstruct a view, so its vertical supports and the railing itself need to be small in profile as well as sturdy.

Finding the right combination of strength and attractiveness for a railing takes some ingenuity. At Wind Whistle, for instance, the vertical supports ("balusters") are spaced four inches apart to give the visual impression that a young child could not possibly slip through; a six-inch spread would do the job, but it would not *look* as secure. Because I wanted to concentrate on the view, I used painted steel balusters rather than wood. I would have had to use a 1½-inch board in wood, but I could get by with only a ⅜-inch square bar in steel. It looks light and decorative, but it is tough as . . . steel.

A final outdoor structure that concerns an architect is the garage. Like it or not, the car must have a home, and it should not be an afterthought, or it will look like one. It may seem simple to design a large box with a single purpose, but garage design is often difficult. The garage has to hold one, two, or more cars—very large, stationary objects—and often bikes, garden equipment, garbage cans, and other paraphernalia as well. It has to be located for easy access; the architect must study angles and grades carefully in order to position the driveway. Here in Minnesota, for example, a steeply inclined driveway is a midwinter terror. If the garage connects to the house, as most of my clients request, the entry should be at a convenient point in the circulation system. No one wants to walk from the garage into a bedroom, the living room, or the bathroom. Actually, it is easier to make the garage appealing if it is a separate and free-standing structure. The space between house and garage can be developed with walls, plantings, walkways, and other design elements.

An architect cannot consider any of these rooms and structures in isolation. Garage, roof deck, bedroom, kitchen, and all the spaces of the house have to be designed with their individual requirements in mind, but they must also form a coherent whole. While designing each room, the architect must also consider how it will fit into his plan and elevation. This "visualization" is one of an architect's essential skills.

Holding all the rooms of a house in my mind and creating an organic and intriguing design is a challenge I enjoy. Maybe that's why I refer to the way I earn my living not as "my business" but as "my game." Like any game, architecture has rules, penalties, and some losses—but it is so fascinating I never get tired of playing.

WHEN IS YOUR HOUSE REALLY FINISHED?

No house is ever really finished. After moving in, an owner will hang pictures, move furniture from one side of the room to the other, and experiment with different room arrangements. Landscaping and planning and planting a garden will take time. After a few weeks or months, an owner may decide on an extra shelf in the storage room, or a workbench next to the laundry facilities, or a curtain on a high window that throws inconvenient light on a computer. A few years pass, and an owner may decide to erase all the dirty fingermarks on the hallway wall with new paint. Or perhaps a teenage daughter simply gets tired of the pale pastels in her bedroom and demands a gloriously loud wallpaper instead. Every house continues to evolve.

When does an architect sign off? Many years ago my teacher, Robert Cerny, lamented that too many architects never finished their projects. He was mainly talking about projects planned for public clients—city, county, and state governments, colleges and universities, hospitals —whose buildings are often promoted by politicians or boards of directors and then used by the public. Bob Cerny felt that too often these clients found themselves with a building that was technically complete but still lacked many finishing details. The architect had departed without leaving any guidelines about landscaping, artwork, furniture placement, or window coverings, or, indeed, without any direction about how the building could best be used. The architect is often the logical coordinator of these details—if he cares and if he is still around.

A house is not usually left so bereft. The owner and architect have established a close and sensitive relationship, if everything has gone mostly right, and most details have been discussed and resolved throughout the process of building the house. A client will tell me, "I've got to have room on that wall for my six-foot grand piano," or ask, "What kind of carpeting do you think I should put in the living room to coordinate with Orientals in the hall?" Often the architect has suggested and engaged a landscape architect to help plan the outdoor environment, and sometimes a client wishes to use an interior designer as well. When the architect leaves, the owner can carry on quite capably.

Contractually, the house is complete when the architect, in writing, approves the client's final payment to the contractor. At this point, the contractor has substantially completed his or her work. Before giving this approval to the client, the architect carefully inspects the finished house and makes a "punch list," an inventory of all items that are incomplete or inadequately completed. Most owners have an eagle eye for such flaws; indeed, some have been making their own punch lists for a long time. (I don't know the origin of this phrase, but, given the natural frustration of clients who see possible flaws in their new dream house, I can guess.) The punch list is submitted to the contractor; it now becomes the document which, when fulfilled, will determine that the house is complete. The architect approves the payment, and the contractor disappears. At this time, the architect submits his or her own final bill.

This last stage in the process of building a house is sometimes a delicate one, fraught with possibilities for misunderstanding and bad feeling (if not punches). All parties need to exercise judgment and a spirit of compromise. I urge my clients not to expect an absolutely perfect house. Building a house is too human an enterprise ever to achieve that. Many, many hands have touched that house, giving it life and individuality, but also leaving a human mark. A specially de-signed and built house should be pleasing, livable, and exciting, but cannot be perfect.

The degree of perfection (or imperfection, depending on one's atti-tude) is what needs negotiation. Most punch-list items concern finish elements—paint, wallcovering, Sheetrock, millwork—rather than basic structure. (No architect who has kept an eye on the job will be faced at this moment with an off-center window, wobbly floor, or tilting chim-ney.) An electrical-outlet plate may not quite cover the hole in the wall cut out for the outlet, for instance, or some lighting fixtures may not have arrived or been installed, or a kitchen-cupboard door may stick.

I certainly do not discount such items as unimportant. They can be irritants that might spoil an owner's pleasure in a new house. Some-times a client wants to move into a house that is substantially complete, one that may even have passed final inspection by building-code officials, but still has a long punch list. I do not recommend this. I myself have moved into several houses yet to be completed, and each time I have sworn I'd never do it again. Even a few missing baseboards require workmen arriving (or not arriving), buzzing drills and flying sawdust, and mess and noise of all kinds—interruptions of privacy and peace that can ruin the first days in the new house.

For my part, I have to be willing to take a stand on what constitutes proper completion. I must consider standards that exist in the con-struction industry and decide whether workmanship meets that stan-dard. Often I am not merely the owner's agent but an arbitrator as well. Once I listened to an owner (whose temper, unfortunately, was quick to ignite and slow to dampen) rage for an hour about a slight defect in the graining of a cabinet. I could not see the defect unless I stood at a certain spot, squinted in a particular way, and waited for just the right light to hit the defect. Though sympathetic with the owner's desire for perfection—it *was* a brand-new cabinet—I knew that to replace it meant to rip out *all* the cabinets, redo all the kitchen millwork, and probably end up with a marred floor, a few nicks and scratches in other places, and a whole new (and much longer) punch list. I bit my lip, held my own temper, listened and replied, and waited until the owner finally decided he could live with the slight misgraining.

A house is generally guaranteed for a year, based on a letter from the architect certifying that the work is complete. That letter should make it clear to everyone when the year is up. The general contractor is responsible for the guarantee, which covers virtually any kind of malfunction, and if there is a problem the general contractor will often call in the appropriate subcontractor. If the heating doesn't work right, for example, the client will call the general contractor, who in turn will call the firm that installed the heating/cooling system. After the punch list is cleared, very little usually goes wrong during that first year. But architects remain on call for much longer than that, whether they like it or not. An irate owner will not hesitate to telephone (at almost any hour) if, for example, he or she discovers water in the basement, a drip from the ceiling, or indeed water anywhere it is not supposed to be.

One of my clients—let's call him Michael—phoned me in great agitation fifteen years after I'd remodeled his house because he thought I was responsible for a sudden leak in his roof. Although my wife rolled her eyes as I left, I hurried over. I soon discovered that the problem stemmed from a much later remodeling job, a small one that Michael had contracted for himself. Although I had not been involved, I suggested how the problem might be fixed, Michael seemed mollified, and I went home.

A few weeks later, after another rainy spell, I walked into a fancy downtown restaurant where (I later gloomily thought) many of my clients and potential clients often eat lunch. As I started toward a table, I heard Michael's loud, distinctive voice booming out. "James!" he called peremptorily. "My roof isn't leaking anymore!" I waved and smiled weakly. No architect wants to be identified in public with a leaky roof. Michael's greeting had the unfortunate ring of "I see you've stopped beating your wife!"

Although Michael tugged a bit on our friendship, I like to keep in touch with my clients. During the first year, and often after that, owners tend not to want to bother me, but I am eager to have them call when questions arise. Often they would like advice on some aspect of design, perhaps a major new piece of furniture, or a color change. I'm gratified when clients seek me out over the years, because each house is special to me. In fact, as I look back on my thirty-some years of design experience, one of more than a few things I'd do differently is to keep in closer touch with my past clients. They are a superb group—relationships with them are not always easy, but always worthwhile.

One of my nicest surprises recently was a call from a new owner —the third—of a house I'd designed twenty-five years before. She seemed as pleased with it as my first client, although she wanted my advice on how best to update and remodel parts of it to adapt to her own special needs. She didn't want to change or interfere with the basic design, she told me, and of course I told her in return that I'd be delighted to give her what help I could. That is what it is all about for an architect: building a house that continues to live far past the date when the first owner moves in.

AT WORK ON WIND WHISTLE

PART TWO

CASTLES IN THE AIR: A CLIENT'S INTRODUCTION

On a cold Saturday morning in early February 1987, James and I stood for the second time on a bluff overlooking Lake Pepin. For several months we had been searching for a secluded spot where we could build a small retreat. I wanted an isolated place to write, read, walk, and recover a sense of connection to the land. After setting a limit of ninety minutes' driving time from our Minneapolis home, we had explored farms on flat prairie land, patchy woods on meandering small rivers, and hilly parcels that would clearly soon become suburban. Nothing seemed right. Then James suggested we look south rather than north, and investigate some land he'd heard was for sale high above the Mississippi at Lake Pepin, where the river widened to three miles below high bluffs.

We saw this particular lot, thought about it, talked it over, and decided to revisit it a week later. A sharp wind sang through the trees, making us both shrink deeper into our down jackets. Sun glinted over small mounds of snow and bounced over the ice-covered lake below with a brilliance that made us blink. I walked toward the ridge, marked by a broken fence from a long-ago farm, and looked through jagged tree branches toward the ice-covered sweep below.

During the past week, I'd worried about noise from the highway that ran four hundred feet beneath the cliff. But today all was quiet. February is not usually a beautiful month in the Midwest, especially when snow has melted or blown away, leaving a brown and ice-patched earth under gray skies. But today was breathtaking on the bluff, as we stood sheltered behind the trees, listening to the whistling wind, breathing in frosty air, letting our minds swoop and soar into the seemingly limitless sky that stretched over Lake Pepin. I was reminded of one of my favorite spots on earth, the seaside cliffs at Mendocino in northern California. I felt the same awe here as I did there. "You know," I said with a hesitation that surprised me, "I think this is too grand for the likes of me."

James laughed. "That settles it," he said, putting his arm around me. "We'll call and make an offer as soon as we get back to the city."

"Do we have to wait?" I asked anxiously. "Couldn't we find a pay phone somewhere?"

He nodded, and we hurried toward the car. We had not been on the site this time much more than ten minutes, but somehow we both knew. This was it.

When we began to talk about the house we'd build, I was excited but a little uneasy. I had never had a house designed for me before, with my own wishes and needs taken into account. "This will be your special place," James assured me. "I'll love it too, but you're my client."

Like any client, I confronted my architect with a grab bag of passions and prejudices. I loved the look of English cottages. I hated stark minimalist houses, the kind designed as a background for gleaming metallic furniture, white futons on the floor, and huge abstract paintings on the walls. In fact, except for the ones James designed, I was wary of most modern houses—too much glass, not enough coziness. A

Victorian at heart, I longed for winding stairs, turrets, hidden cupboards. I had other quirks: I was fond of lying in bed and looking out of windows. I didn't like most carpeting. I abominated beige. I would have to be talked into louvered window blinds. I was very particular about reading light. For rooms, I wanted angles, curves, arches, anything but plain boxes.

How had I acquired all these strong feelings? Every client of an architect has a history of houses, even if it is just one home where he or she has always lived. All my houses have made deep impressions on me. I remember the ones in which I lived happily or unhappily, the rooms I loved or decorated or just endured, the houses I'd wanted to buy but hadn't. All helped form my personal architectural history, a mixture of experience and fantasy.

Since James knew me so well, he didn't need to study my history of houses. He already knew many of my stories and much of my taste. With just a few questions, he was able to design a retreat he knew I'd love. But watching Wind Whistle take shape, first on paper and then in three dimensions, made me review my past in terms of the houses I'd known. What did Wind Whistle represent? Where did it fit in terms of all those other places I'd lived? Why did I love it so?

The more I saw myself in relation to my history with houses, the more I realized how difficult, intuitive, and risky an architect's job is. A client brings a lot of baggage, plastered with labels and claim-check stubs, to the drafting table. The architect often has to guess what is inside those battered satchels and suitcases. To design something that will reflect a client's idiosyncratic tastes and indefinable dreams, the architect sometimes has to proceed as if he or she can see through all that accumulation with an X-ray eye. I wasn't even sure of everything I was carrying.

Once I dreamed of being an architect. Of course, like many young girls years ago, I also dreamed of other careers: nurse, librarian, newspaper reporter. Armed with a medical kit from the Sears Christmas catalog, I knew how to "play nurse"; I sometimes stacked up my small collection of books and played librarian; once, for a three-day run, I even wrote a family newspaper. Playing at being an architect was easiest. All I needed was a pencil and a blank piece of paper, and I was ready to design houses.

As far as I knew, that was what an architect did: design houses. The big buildings in Ames, Iowa—the Iowa State Memorial Union, Ames High School, or Mary Greeley Hospital—were all in place long before I was born, and I couldn't imagine that anyone had actually *designed* them. When the Hy-Vee grocery store went up across from our junior high school, I watched the process with only mild interest, assuming it was being built by a contractor. I respected contractors—when Mr. Twedt built our small rambler in 1950, my mother always spoke of him with irritated deference—but I didn't want to be a contractor. I wanted to be an architect.

So I sketched house plans. A few years ago, I found some of those yellowed scraps of paper, covered with squarish rooms neatly drawn and carefully labeled. I don't seem to have worried much about exteriors, and since I've always lacked an accurate sense of three-dimensional space, I didn't struggle with volume. Instead I concentrated on elaborate groupings of rooms, large interior spaces that flowed into each other. Like many children, I coveted privacy, so my houses were fantasies of escape through successive doors.

As I drew huge bedrooms and spacious porches, Ping-Pong rooms, dressing rooms, studies, and extra bathrooms, I pictured myself walking through these seductive spaces. Sometimes I even sketched in a few pieces of furniture. These imaginary houses were a natural continuation of an earlier childhood pleasure—fashioning hideouts, perhaps under a cloth-covered card table or beneath a large pine tree. But these architectural sketches were not as satisfying as those hideouts. Once I had finished a floor plan, I had no idea what to do next. So I'd try a different floor plan, and then still another. After a while, I ran out of variations, grew bored, and put my sketchbook away. Before long, especially when I realized my older sister was going to be the artist in the family, I surrendered the idea of being an architect.

But I kept dreaming about houses and rooms. One of my first childhood memories is about an imaginary house. When I was three years old, my mother told me a story about tree fairies, magical creatures who lived inside trees. The next day at nursery school, I wandered around the wooded yard, knocking on tree after tree, at first politely, then more insistently. Finally I pounded in rage on one large tree that seemed to me a perfectly logical place for fairies to live. No matter how I knocked and called, no one inside the tree answered. When my mother came to pick me up, I was in tears, and she had to pull me away, gently, before I would consent to listen to her explanation. I didn't care so much that there were, in fact, no tree fairies as that they did not live inside a tree. What I envisioned was a marvelous secret world, a hidden little house, the kind of place where a fairy (or a little girl) could live in safety and splendor. When, several years later, I read about Peter Pan's refuge among tree roots, I envied the house in Never-Never Land more than his ability to fly.

While growing up in two pleasant but quite ordinary houses, I kept searching for romantic alternatives. Next door to us, the Millers' old three-story house had a mysterious unheated attic. On rainy days, kindly Mrs. Miller sometimes let my sister and me climb winding flights of stairs, pass down a long hallway, open unexpected doors, and explore the attic. It stretched invitingly under the eaves into cobwebby corners. We uncovered treasures, like a wicker baby buggy, old photograph albums, and young Eddy Miller's matchbook collection, left untouched ever since he had died in the war. The rain pounded on the roof, we peered out of small windows onto our own roof far below, and I wished I could live in an attic forever.

Modern houses, I learned, didn't have attics. The most "arty" one, just down the block, was a concrete, sort-of-Bauhaus, sort-of-1930s-

Deco structure, built with flat roof, odd terraces, and several levels. When I baby-sat in that house, I was always cold and a little afraid. The gray concrete walls hinted of prison, the large floor-to-ceiling windows in the living room had no curtains, and the dark night with its unseen intruders pressed in upon me. If this was "modern," I didn't want to have anything to do with it.

I didn't think of our own developer's-model rambler as "modern." It was just a house like everyone else's, neither exciting nor romantic. It had no hidden corners or unexplored spaces, no turrets, no screened porches or pantries. My own bedroom was small and square, like all the other rooms. But early in my teens, my voracious reading, which included house-and-home magazines, gave me both hope and inspiration. Romance, I decided, was a question of interior decor. If only I could buy a canopy bed or a kidney-shaped dressing table with a ruffled skirt! At least I could work toward the same effect.

So until I left home for college, I periodically tried to transform my simple small bedroom, with its blue linoleum floor and whitish pine walls, to look more like the rooms in *Better Homes and Gardens* or *House Beautiful*. Mostly I rearranged my four pieces of furniture —bed, chest of drawers, desk, straight-back chair—in their few possible combinations. Once I positioned my flat-topped desk at an angle to the wall, which created an interesting space as it jutted into the center of the room, but I kept bumping my hip against its corner as I tried to get to my dresser. On those days of change, as I heaved and shoved the furniture from one wall to another, I felt like a cross between an interior decorator and a sculptor who worked with large stones. At the end of the morning's work, I was never satisfied.

When I went away to college, and then graduate school in Berkeley, California, I had little choice about my environment. My rooms offered even less scope for imagination than my bedroom at home, and my budget was just as limited. What I mainly remember about my college room was how claustrophobic it seemed. Far from Iowa and desperately homesick for windswept skies, I shoved my metal bedframe underneath my small window. At night, lying on my back, I could see part of a large tree and a few stray stars caught in its branches.

My first chance to find a personal space that suited me came when, at twenty-three, I became engaged. The right apartment seemed a critical element of marriage, and I was prepared to devote as much time to looking at apartments as to studying for my graduate language exams. We were to continue living in Berkeley, and I knew instantly that we had to have a view, as well as plenty of windows, a big kitchen, and a rent under $100 a month, a modest sum even in 1963. I wanted to avoid buildings that were "Danish modern," which meant new buildings with cramped rooms prettified with standardized teak furniture. I wanted to furnish my own apartment. "Modern" still sounded suspect.

As soon as I had passed my qualifying exams, I spent most of my afternoons reading ads or walking the hilly streets behind the university, looking for apartments with views. In the evenings my fiancé drove us to look at possibilities. I remember a large one-room studio on Panoramic Way, with a Murphy bed that folded down from the wall, but, alas, no place for either of us to be alone, and a tiny cottage high in the Oakland hills, ringed on three sides by windows, but offering only one electrical outlet and no window shades. I felt we could plug in our toaster and coffee sequentially, eating breakfast in stages, and change our clothes while crouching on the floor. We had a bitter fight about that cottage.

I kept looking. Perhaps I unconsciously knew that my marriage would be difficult and that I needed a nurturing space, complete with the solace of San Francisco Bay and the Golden Gate Bridge. I was already a convert to Emerson's dictum: "The health of the eye seems to demand a horizon. We are never tired, so long as we can see far enough." When I found a spacious one-bedroom apartment in an older stucco four-plex with a Mediterranean feeling, only $95 a month, and opening onto a full view of the Golden Gate from the dining-nook window, I knew it was just what I'd wanted. Every evening, before I started making dinner, I poured myself a glass of sherry and sat in front of the window, looking at the red-gold gleam of the far-off bridge, the white building blocks of San Francisco, floating banks of fog or moving ribbons of gray rain over the water. My marriage foundered, but my awareness of the importance of the right living space has lasted to this day.

A year later we moved to Minneapolis, where views were scarce. I settled for the second floor of a duplex with an extra bedroom for a shared study. Although I had not yet read Virginia Woolf, I increasingly yearned for a room I could call my own. When we began to house-hunt, I hunted with zest. Since I didn't want something "modern," and my husband didn't like the problems and upkeep of Victorian houses, we sought out buildings from the 1920s and 1930s, which had character and style, usually needed work, and were often affordable. Eventually we bought a small "starter" house, vaguely stucco Mediterranean, and later a much larger and fancier one, English Tudor as reinvented by Scandinavian craftsmen.

I loved both those houses. I learned to appreciate woodwork, whether a carved oak stair railing or paneled doors. In the larger house, I appropriated a room that was almost my own, a small floral-papered adjunct to the bedroom, a porchlike enclosure with wicker furniture and windows on three sides. More than ever, I wanted windows that framed landscapes of trees. Because Minnesota winters are long, I cherished natural light, sunshine that brightens a room even on the coldest days. Without knowing it, I was growing to have a set of assumptions about what I needed in my environment.

I also acquired more experience about what I *didn't* like in houses. Despite my admiration of high ceilings and carpenter's fancies in older houses, I found myself hating their basements. I loved plaster arches and heavy oak doors, but I tired of cracks and fissures, creaking floors, mice, windows that were hard to open, and doors that were hard to close. I still shunned contemporary houses, but I began to wish my favorite older houses had slightly more modern habits. When I met James, I was subconsciously prepared to re-think "modern."

Of course, my history with houses is also a history of relationships. If I were to tell the story of my first marriage, which would be necessarily biased and incomplete, I might be able to frame it in terms of the houses we lived in. I could describe how we decided to buy them, how we worked on and decorated them, how we struggled to dispose of them. I could talk about confrontations over a wallpaper steamer or disagreements about a house one of us loved and the other did not. In a postscript, I might add a chapter about the house I bought for myself after our divorce, where I finally indulged my own independent and somewhat quirky taste. Then I could explain how, when I met James, I immediately loved *his* house, with its casual elegance, cheerful light, and imaginative use of space. On our second date, it piqued my interest in its designer. Three years later, I married him and moved in.

But house stories, like childbirth or fishing stories, are mostly fascinating to the teller. Tales of frustrated house-hunting, archaeological adventures with layers of wallpaper, and anecdotes about the horrors of remodeling leave me yawning. What one person loves about a house can also be inexplicable to another, but most people understand that a house becomes part of its owner's identity. Moving out can become one of life's major traumas.

I do like happy endings, however, and where all my house stories eventually end is at Wind Whistle. As I walk contentedly from room to room, which I often do as soon as we've arrived, I am reminded how much my happiness here derives from my long experience with other houses. Everywhere I see interesting angles, curves, and changing perspectives, reminiscent of the older houses I loved. But Wind Whistle's construction is so close and tight that not a board quivers underfoot, no mildew collects in damp corners, and no rodents lurk below in a murky basement.

As I lie on the living-room sofa or in my bed, I gaze through ample windows into treetops, just as I've always dreamed. The view across the Mississippi is so glorious that I no longer feel wistful about that first apartment overlooking San Francisco Bay. I can also look up through clerestory windows into the sky, the sky I longed for when I was in that cramped college room. With cathedral ceilings and open circulation, Wind Whistle has a sense of roominess. I can stretch here, and even in winter, when severe weather keeps me indoors, I never feel as if I need to pace.

Wind Whistle is also warm and cozy. When a fire crackles in our black wood stove, I curl up under a wool throw and feel quite snug. Although the forms and shapes of Wind Whistle are abstract and unusual, it is a modern house that is neither cold nor stark. With its unexpected color, it even has a sense of humor, a gaiety that never fails to lift my spirits. Since the graining of the wood shows through the stained pine of walls and ceilings and the oak floors have been naturally finished, I can also enjoy the beauty of wood surfaces— just as I did in those 1920s fake-Tudor houses I treasured in my earlier life.

Best of all, the house seems to encircle and protect me. When I climb the stair to my study—that room of my own I've always wanted—I shut my door on the everyday world. With its ladder leading up to the crow's-nest deck and its windows looking both up and down the river on one side and into the garden and woods on the other, my room might feel like home to Peter Pan, if not to a tree fairy. At Wind Whistle I am convinced that I am living in a magical world.

So for this grateful client, the architect was a medium and a magician. I no longer fantasize about being an architect (never during the process of building Wind Whistle did I sketch a single floor plan!), but I feel quite smug about being married to one. Through sympathetic imagination and skill, he called up my past and transformed it into the house of my dreams.

GETTING STARTED

12

A week after Susan and I decided to buy our lot on Lake Pepin, I started the design for Wind Whistle. Unlike most of my houses, this one didn't begin with a pencil. It began with a long-handled lopper. My associate and friend Jim Foran, a young architect in our firm, drove with me to the site, and we spent several hours clearing away brush so we could gauge the incline and also get a sense of how to open up the best views by judicious tree-trimming. Then I started to think about what kind of house belonged there.

Soon I had made a site study. After a discussion with Susan, I knew our "program," what kind and number of rooms we wanted. We would have living/dining/kitchen areas that were separate but spatially inter-active, a master bedroom with a walk-in closet, a bedroom for our daughter, Jenny, or occasional guests, a single bath, a study for Susan, a separate work space for me, a sauna, and a deck area. Based on the program and our budget, I assumed our house would have to be no more than 1,500 square feet of finished enclosed space, a comfortable

115

but not extravagant size. Even if we could have afforded it, we did not plan to have a behemoth on the bluff.

Although I intended my design to be quite special, I wanted it to be quiet, a house that attracted favorable attention without shouting for it. Wind Whistle (a name that came to me one blustery morning as I tramped the site) would be wonderful rather than weird. As I explained in Chapter 6, "Who's Holding the Pencil?," I still like the idea that form follows function, but I've also developed an affection for high spirits, whimsy, color, and just plain exuberance in architecture. Because Susan was my client, I could express all these aspects of design at Wind Whistle.

As I began the design, I was determined to disturb the site as little as possible. After much careful consideration, we trimmed large branches from several trees in order to clear a view, but we needed to remove only one entire tree, a large cedar. Now we are rewarded by the great number of birds who find shelter in the various pines, cedars, and shagbark hickories that surround us.

Respecting the environment did not mean our house had to disappear into it. I have used this disappearing approach in many houses, particularly vacation homes, usually by building with natural unfinished wood and designing a simple profile. (My grown children now share just such a house I designed twenty years ago on the shores of a secluded lake in the great woods of northern Wisconsin. It blends into its surroundings until it almost becomes part of the forest.)

Both the site and the intended character of Wind Whistle, however, called for something less self-effacing. The magnificent view looks down over the Mississippi, one of the world's great rivers, where tugboats pass up and down pushing barges several city blocks long. It encompasses miles of water, hundreds of hills, thousands of trees, and tons of rock. Eagles and vultures soar just a few yards overhead. Wind Whistle did not want to be "tucked away"; it demanded to assert itself a little.

I also considered Susan's wish, a Midwestern version of an English cottage, simple, cozy, and welcoming. She had also spoken longingly of color inside and out, the bright and cheerful effect that English gardens bring to the rustic tones of their cottages. "Lemon yellow, grass green, sky blue," she ticked off on her fingers. "We don't get much color in Minnesota in the winter. I'd like to have it in my house." Since we are both of Norwegian ancestry and our house would sit above the tiny Scandinavian town of Stockholm, I thought approvingly of the warm palette used so successfully by Swedish artist Carl Larsson. The design, materials, and colors for Wind Whistle began to take shape in my mind.

The shape and plan, or "footprint," of Wind Whistle went through many changes. In its final form, the footprint is based on a repeated octagonal shape, though the exterior is more complex, with its varying rooflines from the cliffside gables to the undulating slope over Jenny's room. It meets the criteria I had set for myself as a designer. It has 1,420 square feet, well within my first proposed size. Built of common materials and by common construction methods, it stretched but did not break our budget. It is a sheltering retreat, a place for study and repose, and a delightful vacation home, and it never fails to lift our spirits when we enter it.

How did all this happen? I sketched and thought, drew some more and thought some more, retraced over an old design and developed it, abandoned an idea and tried again. I include here a short series of sketches to illustrate my early attempts to follow the program and intentions I've outlined above. These sketches are not exhaustively complete. No architect, unless perhaps he or she confidently expects world fame, saves, let alone dates all abandoned drawings.

Many of my first ideas (Figures 6, 7, 8, 9, 10) emerged simply as manipulations of form, almost like finger exercises. In fact, my fingers do get itchy until I have a block of time I can set aside to work intensively on a house design. I use these first sketches as a creative outlet.

Beyond therapeutic value, these sketches show what I might call "predesign." I nicknamed (6) "The Bastille"; it is a high fortress, a kind of watchtower on huge pillars. (I must admit it is not very inviting.) I wanted to be certain not to forget that Susan had spoken about an English cottage, so (7) is a determined effort to envision one. This house did not relate to the cliff at all, though it did sit well among the woods and meadow behind. Pursuing the same country-cottage style,

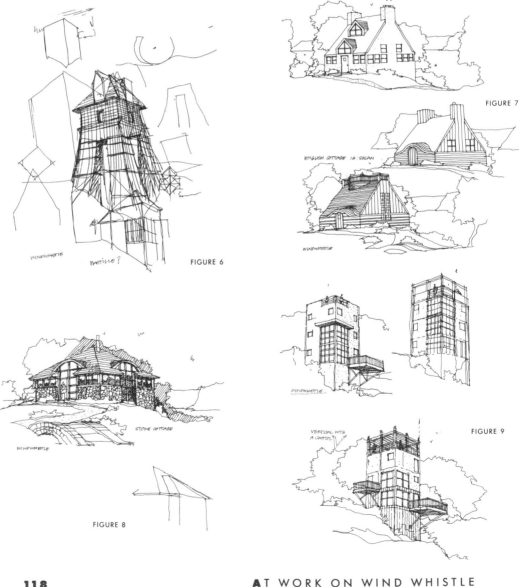

FIGURE 6

FIGURE 7

FIGURE 8

FIGURE 9

in (8) I used a heavier stone base, tying the house to the ground, and I tried a less dominant roofline.

Since many of my smaller houses have been vertical, I naturally began considering Wind Whistle from the aspect of the bluffs. (9) shows a simple vertical shape in three slightly different expressions. In each, I envisioned at least one interior room to rise the full height of the space. The little dots on the facade suggest a very rough stucco. Note that one house has just a roof deck, the second has a roof deck and balcony, and the third has three decks, including a sheltered, trellised rooftop that would have been quite lovely. But the rest of the house didn't please me, so the rooftop had to be abandoned. Parts of one design are often not transferable to another one.

Sketch (10) continues the same vertical theme, but I carved away parts of the pure form to create a more cubistic (and possibly more interesting) exterior shell. Some architects might call this "exploding the shell" and letting the parts resettle. This design would have given me much more freedom than (9) in planning my interior spaces.

My first truly productive study, (11), is what I call a "test" of the program on a site. This is always my initial stage in real design, as opposed to playful sketches. I use the word "test" to indicate a first cut, not usually a lasting plan, a design that simply fits the size of the house to the site and takes into account the views, slopes, sun, and other aspects of the site study. This first design gives me a sense of how a house of the appropriate size will fit onto a site, and perhaps what kind of shape and forms will work best there.

My test for Wind Whistle (11) stretches all the rooms along the view, with a screened porch at one end and a master bedroom at the other. It is an obvious and logical plan. A simple roof covers this lineup of rooms. Although I labeled this drawing as "nice but dullsville," I can see that it does bear a resemblance to the house I finally built. That resemblance reminds me that from the first handshake with a new

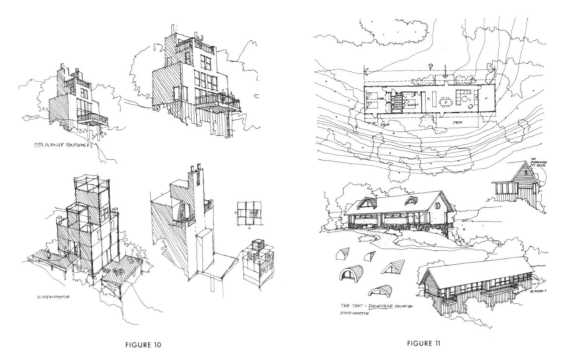

FIGURE 10

FIGURE 11

client (or, in this case, from Susan's first excited comments), vague ideas and impressions begin forming in my mind. They will emerge later at some point in the design process, somehow influencing a design to make it just right for this particular house. Somewhere in (11) is a germ of Wind Whistle that was probably there from the beginning.

I developed this test further in (12). Shortening the house and putting the guest bedroom on the meadow side, I found, made the plan look a little less like one of the trains that travel below our bluff. It was, I noted at the time, "an improvement," but the design still seemed rather bland. The connection between the bedroom roof and the study roof remained unresolved, although I had gotten rid of the rather silly gables. Even in these early sketches, I made some preliminary notes about where to place furniture.

In (13), I pulled out all the stops. This was clearly my cliffside Shangri-La. I was so entranced by it I even asked Jim Foran to commit it to watercolor so I could admire it better. The living area, located in the center, would have had a phenomenal view, and the interior space of this area would have been superb. The studio space is below (not an

OVERLEAF: The living room is the heart of the house, a place to read and relax, make music or listen to it, and entertain friends. From the window at the right, a long view opens out over Lake Pepin. The window to the left brings the surrounding woods into the room as well.

OPPOSITE: When a house has more than one level, it is important to have a viewing point where you can survey the space. Here we look out onto the lofty ceilings of the living area.

ABOVE RIGHT: The wood-burning stove, visible from the dining area, is an important symbol of heat and comfort. Several different kinds of wood surfaces are juxtaposed here, from white-oak floors to the matching walls, above which rough-sawn fir beams lead to a ceiling surface of pine boards.

BELOW RIGHT: The octagonal dining room projects into the outdoors and allows windows on three sides. The high window just visible to the left is an important part of the natural lighting. Without it, the soaring ceilings would seem dark. These ceilings are also softened by the gentle blue stain, suggesting the color of the sky.

BELOW: The living area is removed from the rest of the house not only by visual distance but by level, since it is sixteen inches lower than the dining area. Yet the space seems continuous, which creates a feeling of flow and an illusion of even more room.

LEA BABCOCK

LEA BABCOCK

LEA BABCOCK

ABOVE: Susan wanted a room that would reflect her own taste and personality. She chose creamy plaster walls as a background for her favorite posters and photographs. The pink work surface is echoed by the rosy stain on the wood ceiling and window trim, a tone also picked up in the Persian rug.

BELOW: The focal point of this room is obviously the dining table, designed of Mankato Kasota stone (and weighing more than 900 pounds!). The red V-groove cut into the top is the only decorative element; the beautiful graining of the natural stone provides surface interest. Like the stone sideboard, the table is set on sturdy legs of painted steel.

OPPOSITE: The furnishings in the master bedroom were kept as simple as possible, so that the outside views and the interior natural light command all attention. A walk-in closet next door holds clothes storage, so the only furniture besides the beds and a chair are a wall cabinet and a built-in bookcase (not visible).

BELOW: Here is everything this architect could want in a private study: an ample slanted desk, paper, pen, pencil, T-square, and triangle, all set in an inviting space well supplied with both natural and artificial light, and a great view.

ABOVE RIGHT: From her bed, Jenny looks out onto the garden and woods from this window and onto the meadow from her oval window (seen below and opposite). Linking the room to the garden outside, framed prints of Georgia O'Keeffe's flowers hang on three walls. The wood paneling above her bed is stained a soft green to add to the garden mood.

BELOW RIGHT: The interior curved wall of Jenny's room is covered in a Swedish wallpaper decorated with lavish peonies. In midsummer, this oval window frames a view of a colorful array of lilies, zinnias, baby's breath, petunias, and achillea.

OPPOSITE: Jenny's bedroom fits under the swooping overhang at the front of the house. Her room has a hidden quality, achieved by making it accessible only by a short staircase down from the main living level. Everything in this room fits its smaller proportions.

OPPOSITE: Nature provides brilliant color in western Wisconsin in winter, with blazing blue skies, snow so white it makes one blink, and dark evergreens that stand out vividly against their background. Manmade structures, especially of weathered wood siding, can fade into dullness under such conditions; Wind Whistle sparkles.

ABOVE RIGHT: From the small deck off the master bedroom, we can enjoy a full moon or peer into the trees to see cardinals and blue jays bright against the winter snow. The corner seen here marks the transition between the color on the meadow side (yellow) and a less noticeable color (soft green) on the bluff side.

BELOW RIGHT: This perspective shows how the geometry of the house plays against the romantic curves of the front elevation. It also gives a clear view of the cedar-shingled roof, whose sweeping lines, color, and texture are easily enjoyed from ground level. This early afternoon picture illustrates how Wind Whistle changes its mood with the time of day and the changing season.

OVERLEAF: Hugging the ground on the meadow side, the house has a solid, almost traditional feeling. Note how the curve over Jenny's bedroom echoes the curve of the land. Although this picture does capture a brief faraway vista to the left, it gives no hint of the surprising sharp drop on the other side.

BELOW: On a late summer afternoon, the main deck is shaded by trees on the bluff side. Downriver the sun still lights up mile after mile of the Mississippi. The deck table, of Mankato Kasota stone with painted steel legs, is an unshakable (and utterly immovable) pleasant place for outdoor dining.

ABOVE RIGHT: This view from the sauna deck illustrates the rural side of the site: grassy meadow, garden, and woods that edge the meadow. Note the carpenter's careful finish: the siding of the door is perfectly aligned with the adjacent siding on the wall, so the door is almost unnoticeable from the ground below.

CENTER RIGHT: The deck is a very important part of Wind Whistle. Here we can sense the full panorama of the river below and the sky above. The deck juts directly into the trees. One tree brushes the deck so closely that our strictly indoor cats have to be restrained from making an all-too-logical transition to the outdoors.

BELOW RIGHT: This view of Wind Whistle shows the aerial nature of the site. Steep wooded cliffs drop straight downward from the deck. As one looks up at the house, the dramatic gable above the deck is meant to give a sense of wings. The soaring roof emphasizes the solidity of the lower part of the house.

OPPOSITE: Parts of the roof are often visible, as here from the sauna deck. The form of the roof, the careful fitting of the shingles at every joint, the attractive texture of shingles contrasted to the smooth paint of the railing, and the still further contrast of the slanting wood decking below, all provide visual pleasure.

OPPOSITE: The rainbow-colored roof of the garden house brings color to the glade and meadow even when the garden is not in bloom.

TOP LEFT: The side of the garden house visible from the meadow and entry path is marked by a shed door stained in lavender-blue and outlined in the same bright pink used as a trim color on the main house.

TOP RIGHT: The interior of the garden house also repeats the color scheme of the main house. Both sides are joined visually on the interior by a cathedral ceiling of blue-stained pine boards.

ABOVE: The tepee was added to the meadow both for visual interest and for a certain historical recall, since this area was Native American land for a very long time.

CHRISTIAN KORAB

ABOVE: The sloping lavender tower seen here on the meadow side of the house encases the stairway to the sauna and its small adjacent roof deck or "crow's nest." Apple green edges the swelling curve of roof over the spare bedroom. Note the contrasting texture of the siding on the tower and the roof shingles.

RIGHT: The front door was a true collaboration. James's idea of abstract strokes of color was turned into a sketch by Tom Jenkinson, a student working in his office, and painter Grant Frerichs interpreted the sketch with verve. He used all the colors that had been applied to the house: yellow, green, deep pink, and lavender-blue.

BELOW: The gardens at Wind Whistle are very informal masses of bright flowers, mostly old-fashioned perennials like day lilies, iris, coneflowers, daisies, bleeding hearts, and coralbells. This picture shows the early stages of our garden next to the house.

CHRISTIAN KORAB

CHRISTIAN KORAB

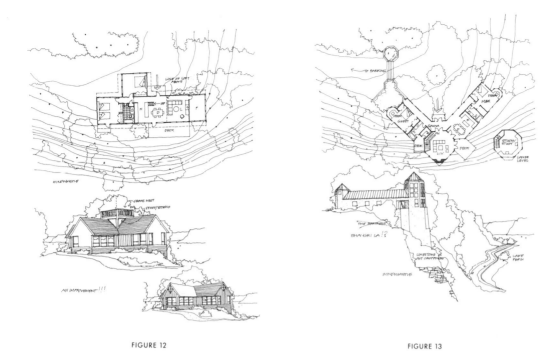

FIGURE 12   FIGURE 13

upper aerie, as Susan had requested), but it too has a downriver view.

So why didn't (13) work? It needed a massive stone base to tie it to the bluff, both physically and aesthetically. With deep excavation, complex scaffolding, carefully engineered connection of the stone to the cliff, and the expensive labor of expert stonemasons, that base would have absorbed half our budget. (A concrete-block base would have been less expensive, but it would have had a jarring relationship to the natural limestone cliffs. And in this setting poured concrete with the right finishes would have been virtually as expensive as stone.)

Just as important, the two wings that recede from the cliffside in (13) also recede from the view. They would not have had their fair share of the glories of the river. Finally, I knew that the spirit of the house was not what we wanted. Susan had asked for a cozy cottage, not a Wisconsin version of San Simeon. But I didn't give up right away. I made an overlay to try to alter the design. It still wasn't right: too big, too expensive, just Too Much.

In (14) I returned to a fairly simple shape in a vertical scheme, but with more complex form than, say, (9). The rooms are very well oriented to the view, dining room in one direction and kitchen in another, with the living room between looking both ways. The upper level wasn't fully developed, but I knew it would fit. This was the first all-shingle drawing, and I liked the idea of moving from wall to roof in one material. But even though I liked its modest nature, the house didn't seem to respond to the bluff. It would have worked better on a relatively level lot.

I moved quickly on to the idea in (15), which is rather a hybrid between vertical and horizontal shapes. It returns to the octagonal idea first studied in (13). In (16) I clarified the idea and then discovered it didn't serve my purposes. The plan has no showstopper. From the outside it still has the massive look I'd rejected earlier. It reminded Susan of a vaguely Frenchified chateau, and that is a long way from an English cottage. From long experience, I could also tell it too would be too expensive to construct.

Ah, (17). I wrote earlier that an architect has to allow himself the liberty to put down even the dumbest idea, as well as smart ones. This is a good example of a dumb idea. Although the plan is not at all bad,

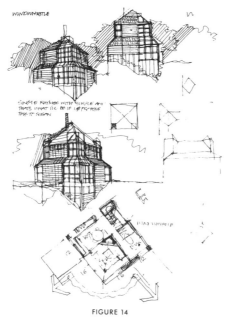

FIGURE 14

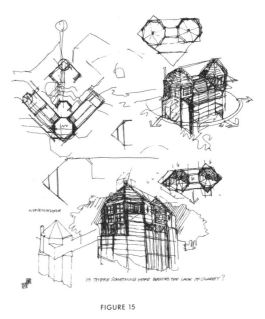

FIGURE 15

FIGURE 16

FIGURE 17

FIGURE 18

since the rooms work well with each other and with the view, the enclosure—what anyone sees from the outside—is embarrassingly overdone. I get a little giddy looking at all the forms, the half-curves turning into sharp gables, lines going up and down and here and there, busy little changes all along the roofline. But I would never have known this if I had worked only on a floor plan. (Notice, however, that the octagonal idea remains, and this will eventually prove to be progress.)

Now I began to refine the octagonal module and to simplify the form of the enclosure. In (18), the octagon is carried into the roofline, which then has consistency from one module to the next. Picking up an idea from an earlier sketch (14), I now also brought the wood shingles down from the roof to the walls. My practiced eye told me that this design would not be difficult to build and would fit into our projected budget.

Looking back at the sketches to date, I decided that the idea expressed in (12) was clear and strong, more appealing than most of the more complex ideas. I spent more time developing this concept into (19). Now I studied a vaulted ceiling, an idea I had toyed with on an earlier cabin design for another site. It would have meant a rounded top to the structure, a combination of copper and wood shingles on the roof, and horizontal wood siding on the walls. I liked what I saw enough to have a model made of it.

The model is shown in (20). (Test models do not attempt to indicate much about the environment. They are studies in form, not a realistic picture of the completed whole. But in this model a few poles show siting of major trees.) I soon found, however, that this house was not going to be feasible for us. I conferred with a builder and with a roofer about how to achieve the vaulted roof. I wanted to have the same form show up inside. In other words, I did not want to put one roof on the outside and construct a different kind of ceiling inside. I learned that this roof would be technically very difficult and therefore expensive. I could not use all shingles to cover an exterior vaulted roof, because it would not have been watertight, yet combining copper and wood would also be difficult and expensive.

So I revised the roof form. I refined the plan further, eliminating the screened porch, which blocked our view from the living room downriver, and extending the octagonal module into the dining area. The changed roof form allowed me to create an upper small deck, a kind of crow's nest, and to locate the sauna where I'd always wanted it, just off a deck (the crow's nest), where I could step immediately

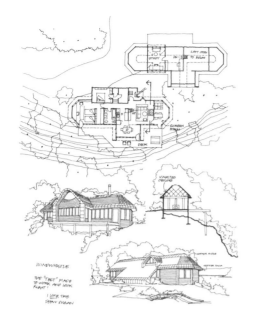

FIGURE 19

FIGURE 21

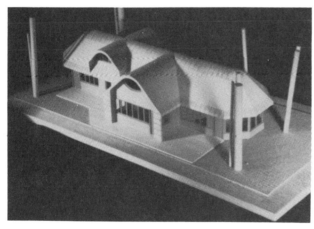

FIGURE 20

out from the sauna into fresh cold air. This design is shown in (21).

The final test of the form was a model shown in (22). This was a model that I tore apart many times in order to try out a variety of refinements to the entire enclosure, such as the peaked dormers, the curved portion of the roof over Jenny's room, the sauna-stairway enclosure opening onto the upper deck, and different kinds of deck on the bluff side. The sad remnants of this model show how much I played with it.

Finally I arrived at (23), which illustrates almost exactly Wind

FIGURE 22

FIGURE 23

Whistle as it was finally built. The plan (24) was made after the house was complete. The cross section (25) shows the spatial characteristics of the rooms and how the rooms relate to each other.

The final site plan (26) was developed after consultation with our landscape architect, Herb Baldwin. It plots a path leading from the parking area through a wooded glade, giving glimpses of the house, to a slight turning marked by large cobblestones on the path, on through a canopy of trees to the first full view of the house.

Now that we have been living in Wind Whistle for more than a

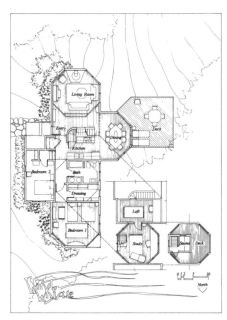

FIGURE 24

FIGURE 25

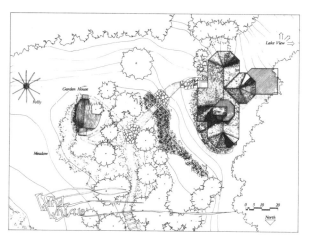

FIGURE 26

year, its design feels both permanent and inevitable. The house almost seems to have grown organically on its site, without any possibility that it might have been different in size or shape or color. When I showed Susan my collection of sketches as we were preparing this chapter, she laughed and shook her head in disbelief at most of them. "Imagine!" she said. That, of course, is what an architect loves to do. Imagining, trying out different ideas, is the way a house gets started. But when the sketching stops, the architect's work has only just begun.

BACK TO THE BOARDS: DESIGN DEVELOPMENT

When Susan had "signed off" on the design, I was ready to start intensive design development. "Signing off" has both a literal and a figurative meaning. Many architects ask their clients to sign and date the design drawings as verifiable evidence of acceptance, in case later the client says, "Hey! That's not what I wanted! Do it all over again, or give me my money back!" Since I always feel that my owners and I understand each other very well by this time, I've never found it necessary to have such a document. For me, "signing off" is verbal approval of the basic design.

As I mentioned in Chapter 7, "The Design Process," design development is a critical stage of the process. At Wind Whistle, I faced many decisions about the structure before I could begin on working drawings. What kind of foundations, wood or concrete or concrete block? What kind of structural framing? Should I use standard lumber or manufactured beams and trusses? How would the various planes and materials meet? Would any of my forms be difficult to build? If so, what details would I need to provide to assist the builders? What kind of operating windows should I specify—double-hung, casement, slider, or fixed? Painted or metal-clad? Special sizes or catalog items? What window manufacturer? These and many other questions needed workable and efficient answers.

The first step after Susan signed off was to confer with my structural engineer, Jack Meyer. I needed his advice to determine the exact framing system for the house. I had decided to use treated wood footings and foundations (see Chapter 14, "The Construction Process," for a description of this part of the structure). The span of the floors would be sixteen feet (the dimensions to the outside of the wall), fairly minimal, so Jack and I could easily plan the joists to provide a sturdy floor with minimum "give." (I don't like my floors to have any bounce, which can sometimes even cause glasses to rattle in the kitchen cupboard.) With a sixteen-foot span, 2×12-inch fir joists sixteen inches apart would work well. (This measurement is called "sixteen inches on center," because the distance is measured from the center of one joist to the center of the adjoining joist.)

That sixteen-foot span might have been even shorter if I had not shown my early plans to my old friend and fellow architect Leonard Parker. For compactness and economy, I had originally wanted to limit the size of the house to a fourteen-foot room width, but Leonard, with his usual directness, had looked at me sternly and said, "Hell, no, James! You absolutely have to add two more feet or you're going to feel cramped." In design development, as in other stages, an architect is trained to learn from other architects, and I listened to Leonard.

The roof system was harder to figure out than the floor framing. I wanted the interior surface to follow the same lines as the exterior, with no trusses and no false ceiling. In a surprising number of houses, a soaring outside roof is no guarantee of high spaces inside. Some architects and developers solve their structural problems by adding trusses that have to be disguised with a dropped or flat ceiling, a sad waste of spatial possibilities.

Jack and I had to be sure that the framing system for Wind Whistle would support the natural outward thrust of the pitched roof. This thrust was intensified by my design, which called for octagonal forms at both ends and in the dining area, with triangular windows set quite high in each of the octagons. (To illustrate the power of this thrust, think of the stone buttresses of Gothic cathedrals. A house is much simpler, but the problem is the same.) With Jack's skill and experience, we worked out the details that would achieve what an architect calls "structural integrity," meaning that the house would not fall down.

Next I talked to my mechanical engineer, Leif Erickson. As these consultations about design development prove, an architect does not produce his or her final, detailed construction drawings unaided or in isolation. Over the years, an architect usually learns which structural and mechanical engineers are inventive and reliable and uses them again and again. They become friends as well as colleagues. (When Susan and I married, we discovered that she had once taught Leif's daughter, and the Ericksons arranged a beautiful bouquet to be delivered to our honeymoon house in Arizona. So Wind Whistle, as a collaborative effort, reached back into Susan's past as well as mine.)

I wanted Leif to help me determine how much heating I needed at Wind Whistle and what type I should select. Normally I make the mechanical contractor on the job responsible for the heating and cooling system. I write performance specifications—what norms the heating and cooling system must satisfy—and let the contractor lay out the system, subject to my approval. I do need to be sure that the grills and ductwork do not affect the aesthetic character of the house. Even though the days of ugly freestanding radiators have passed into design (or nondesign) history, an architect still has to cope with a complex system of metal ducts that have to carry the heat or cool air from the furnace to each room. That ductwork can turn up in some awkward places, and the architect has to reroute, disguise, or hide it.

Because Wind Whistle was in a rural setting and I had not worked with the mechanical contractor before, I felt more secure asking Leif to calculate heat loss and make a layout that would distribute the right amount of heating to the right places. Since we were not planning central air conditioning, which requires ductwork, we could use electric baseboard heating, which is easy to control. Then we pored over Leif's catalogs to find baseboard heaters that were as unobtrusive as possible. Even the ones we finally chose were not things of beauty, and I eventually had them painted sky blue to make them seem less blatantly metallic.

After a year of western Wisconsin's mercurial weather, which varies in temperature from thirty degrees below zero to a hundred above, I was pleased (though not surprised) to find that my engineers had done their work well. Even when the fiercest winds blow over the lake, the house is so stable that it does not shake. (Midwestern storms, which can be quite alarming, are even more unsettling when your house begins to tremble.) During winter when the temperature plummets, we stay cozy. On the hottest summer days, our two room air conditioners, one in the main bedroom and the other in the dining room, keep the heat from being oppressive.

Once these two major engineering tasks had been completed, I proceeded with other aspects of design development. I began to select specific materials. For the roof, I chose cedar shingles rather than asphalt. Since we would be walking so close to the roof—it comes down literally to eye level over Jenny's room, for example—I wanted the texture and character of wood. Asphalt shingles, which are much cheaper, are sometimes unfairly maligned as *looking* cheap; in fact, they come in many pleasing colors and can look quite elegant. But for Wind Whistle, only wood would do.

For the exterior of the house, I chose six-inch redwood lap siding, to be painted, and redwood soffits (the underside of the roof overhang), to be left unpainted. Just as we see the roof quite close, we also look up to the soffits from several vantage points. I wanted to see weathering redwood rather than painted plywood. Now I have to keep a stern eye on Susan's methods of watering her garden, because she sometimes sets her sprinkler dangerously close to those beautiful soffits. (Since they are unpainted, they will waterspot easily.) "If you get water under the overhang on those soffits, the stains will never come out!" I call out the window. Usually she moves the sprinkler. Sometimes she makes me come outside and move it. But so far, the soffits are safe.

Windows come in several styles. I selected outswinging casements, rather than vertical or horizonal sliding windows, because they give the maximum ventilation for any given window area. Especially in the summer, breezes moving through the house are essential for the real flavor of a weekend retreat in the woods. I wanted as much cross-ventilation as possible. But in winter, the windows need to be tightly sealed. The metal-clad wood windows I chose are known for their thermal performance, as well as neat detailing and easy maintenance.

For the interior materials, I began by specifying #2 grade pine, which has some knots, for all the ceilings, except in Jenny's room (the guest room). In a different kind of house I might have used clear pine or a hardwood like white oak, but at Wind Whistle I wanted a certain rustic effect. In Jenny's room, I thought that trying to make our ¾-inch-thick pine boards curve to fit the ceiling surface would be too difficult, so I specified Sheetrock instead. Since then, I have learned that we could have used ⅜-inch-thick pine boards, tongue-and-groove, that would have bent easily. If I were starting all over, I'd probably try for that curve, although the creamy-white ceiling in Jenny's small bedroom does have a light, bright feeling.

For most of the floor and wall surfaces, I chose white oak boards, finished naturally, which means a clear varnish rather than a dark stain. (I have always preferred white oak to red oak for the former's finer grain and lighter color.) Trim would also be of oak. "Trim" refers to all the places where surfaces meet, the various corners and connections that have to be covered with an additional piece of wood. Though it may be a stylish touch, trim is usually functional; fancy molding serves to hide some rough edges and connections.

I had to decide how to treat the interior of the wood windows as well. These windows are usually made of the nicest kind of pine with an attractive grain, and although many people paint or stain them, I like to apply a plain clear varnish and let the wood do its own decorating. When it is varnished, the pine is almost the same color as white oak, so it blended into the color scheme of Wind Whistle very well.

For our interior doors, I chose solid pine for the bedrooms and baths, and louvered pine for storage rooms and closets. A closet can get stuffy when it is shut tight all day, and louvers give privacy while they provide ventilation. All these doors were to be painted in the same hues as the stained ceilings, and the trim around them would match the pine of the ceilings as well.

The wall boards could have run either horizontally or vertically. I chose to make them horizontal, since they could be nailed into the vertical studs much more easily. Like many technical decisions, this had a design aspect as well. The horizontal boards create a subtle encircling effect, which coordinates with the many curving surfaces of Wind Whistle.

Connections offer design challenges, since, as I mentioned above in the case of trim and moldings, these joining places have to be covered in some way. Where our pine ceiling met oak-board walls, I borrowed an idea from another architect, Tom Meyer, a former student of mine who is now an accomplished designer. In one of his recent houses, I had admired a simulated ("simulated" is a word an architect prefers to "fake") 2×12-inch beam that ran continuously just above the window and door frames throughout the house. Of resawn construction-grade fir, Tom's beam had a rough texture that takes stain well. To further the illusion that the beam served a structural purpose, Tom had used ⅝-inch black-painted bolts and washers to hold the beam to the walls. The black was a piquant decorative touch. That too went into the beams at Wind Whistle!

Only a few years ago, along with Tom and other like-minded architects, I would have scorned such license. A beam that isn't a structural element? A "simulated" (read "fake") anything? Yet now I see obsession with "purity" and "honesty of expression" (two key concepts among modernists) as unduly restrictive. I loved Tom's idea, and he was glad to let me borrow it, which didn't surprise me. Most architects learn about artistic generosity as they work together on projects in a studio or an office, a collaborative effort in which each person contributes to the success of the final design.

Not every wall at Wind Whistle would be oak boards. In Jenny's room, the hall, and the bathroom, the walls are Sheetrock (a brand name of gypsum wallboard). Although this was primarily a cost-saving measure, it turned out to offer decorating possibilities. A few years ago, I would no more have used wallpaper in a room than I would have used a simulated beam. But, under Susan's influence (she is as addicted to patterns as she is to color), I began with a marvelously inventive, Oriental-floral-arabesque paper in part of our addition to the Minneapolis house—and I was quite prepared to let Susan search out some wallpaper for Wind Whistle.

What she found was a group of Swedish floral designs in a hand-screened vinyl wallcovering ("wallcovering" is the current fancier term for "wallpaper," and this was certainly more elaborate and expensive than the simple but prosaic wallpaper I used to know). In Jenny's room, large rose-and-green peonies cover the curving wall; in the bathroom, pink tulips with flaring green stems on a white ground enliven the room; and on one wall in the main bedroom, just over the bed and only visible from inside the room, the same pattern of tulips, though with yellow flowers, blooms quite cheerily. All these flowers add to the spirit of Wind Whistle, with its gay interior colors and its surrounding flower gardens outside.

As part of design development, I laid out the furniture to scale on my plans. Since our spaces were fairly small, I had to be sure everything fit comfortably and with good proportions. When we shopped for the few pieces we needed (see Chapter 15, "Finishing Touches"), I was able to tell Susan exactly how big our sofas could be, for example, and how we could arrange them. When she asked about the possibility of buying a small secondhand piano, I saw by glancing at my plan that we would have just enough room on one wall of the living room to accommodate one. It had to be a console, not a grand, and it had to have an ebony finish to match the black stove. Susan had no trouble with these conditions, and now the room has the handsome addition of a piano, which gives us both pleasure when she plays it.

The wood-burning stove was the critical element in the developed design of the living room. Once it was in place, it could not be moved, so everything else would have to be planned around it. I studied all the brochures and material on stoves in our office library, and I wrote away for more, but I still did not see anything that appealed to me. Too many stoves were functional but ugly. Finally I noticed a house featured in an architectural magazine that showed a picture of a room with a stunning Danish black stove of just the size and shape I wanted. Since the magazine published the architect's name, I could and did quickly locate her and call her up. She gave me the manufacturer's name, and the stove was soon on its way. Evidently attractive wood-burning stoves are not easy for anyone to find; when Wind Whistle was featured in another architectural magazine, I got several calls from architects wanting to know where to get "that stove"!

At about this stage, I also designed the stone dining-room table and the wall buffet or serving counter. (Sometimes I do custom-design simple tables, cabinets, and shelving for my clients, though I do not try my hand at any other furniture.) I mapped out the kitchen, showing each appliance (refrigerator, sink, range, microwave oven, and trash compactor) and selected the kitchen cabinets. Susan chose the apple-green Formica for the counters. Then I laid out the bathroom, a basic tub, toilet, bidet, and sink. In the bathroom I put the hot-water heater and pressure tank and located the kitchen sink to back on the bathroom wall. In a pinch, we could always shut down the heat in the rest of the house and just heat this one room to keep the pipes from bursting. My one regret was not being able to specify an extra-long bathtub, a luxury I revel in; the necessary location of corridor and walls limited available space.

All this planning had to be completed before I could begin my working drawings. Although I consulted Susan, my client, on choices like the color of kitchen counters and size of a piano, I was responsible for virtually all the other decisions. Most of my clients, like Susan, have neither the knowledge nor the interest in detail to choose, say, redwood versus plywood soffits. "If I'm asked for an opinion on something, I usually have one," she confessed to me, "so don't ask me unless it's really necessary." We were both happy with the process and its results.

When design development was as complete as I could make it, I had still left a few things undecided. I wasn't yet sure of the shape of the deck and its railing detail, but I knew I could add this last. It was time to get the working drawings underway.

When I begin construction documents, I work separately from my client for a time. Good-bye, Susan! For a while, she could participate only by asking eagerly, "How are the drawings going?" I was on my own, doing a part of the job I've always enjoyed. I'm pleased when I am able to find time in my schedule to do the required drawings and specifications by myself. Although it may sound tedious, this technical phase of the work is hard and challenging. These documents, what we call "a set of working drawings," have to be clear, logical, technically feasible, cost-effective, and consistent with the vision

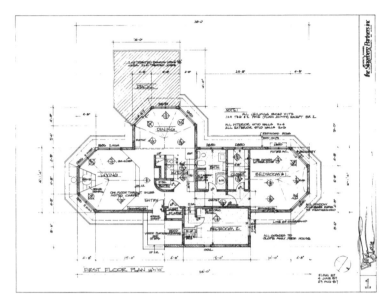

FIGURE 27

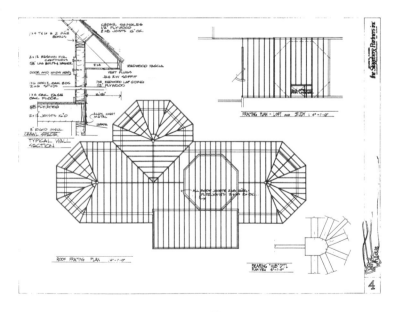

FIGURE 28

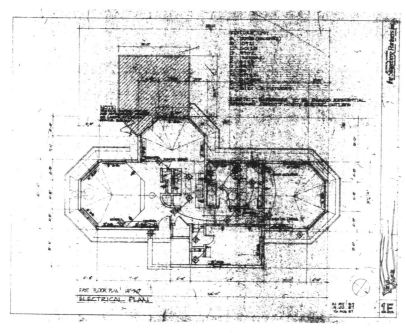

FIGURE 29

shown in the design drawings. I've had other architects who run sizable offices complain that with all their administrative responsibilities, they no longer can take time to do working drawings. Like me, they find it very satisfying to see a project through this stage.

I reproduce here three sample working drawings from Wind Whistle to show what such drawings look like (Figures 27, 28, and 29). Compared to many of my colleagues, I am not a meticulous draftsman, but I do work quickly. I have had so much experience with houses that I can make decisions and implement them easily, an acquired talent that I like to think compensates for my less-than-perfect "hand." (Most architects would love to be known for having "a great hand," even though they know their work requires much more than that.)

Like most architects, I worked on these construction documents for Wind Whistle from the bottom up, drawing and giving dimensions for the footing and foundation plan. After I had drawn up this plan, I laid a clean sheet of "trace" (vellum tracing paper) over the plan and drew the first-floor plan with correct dimensions. I did the same with the loft level and then with the top roof deck. Before I added much information to these plan drawings, I made prints of each for later use; these prints would eventually be the base drawings for the electrical plan.

Next I did two section drawings, one across the narrow part of the house and the other through the middle along the length of the house. A section cuts right through the walls and roof to reveal what is inside. This drawing shows the builder aspects of the structure that are not described by other drawings or written specifications —the height of the ceilings with the exact construction of the peak, for example.

Since I use a scale of ¼ inch equals one foot on these sections, I cannot always describe all the necessary detail. So I select certain parts of the sections to be blown up to a larger scale that allows room for full explanation. One such blowup was the place where the overhang of shingles comes down to the eave and where the eave meets the underside of the soffit.

After the section drawings, I did all the floor and roof framing plans. Then I drew the four "elevations" (Figures 30, 31, 32, 33), one-dimensional frontal drawings of each of the four major sides of the house. These elevations described the exterior form, located and specified the windows, and indicated all the necessary materials. When Susan looked over our set of drawings, these exterior elevations gave her the closest sense so far of what the house was actually going to look like.

Moving from outside to inside the house, I then drew the interior elevations. Here I had to decide which walls required more information and what scale I needed for complete instructions. For plain walls, which had to show only a minimal level of detail, I used a small scale; for walls with bookshelves or other cabinets, I chose a

FIGURE 30

FIGURE 31

FIGURE 32

FIGURE 33

larger scale. Throughout the drawing process, the architect works for as much clarity as possible.

Not every drawing is final. I worked out a complex plan for our deck, a triangular shape that was cantilevered from the house with an intricate structural system. As the house took shape, I could see that the deck was unnecessarily complicated. See Chapter 14, "The Construction Process," for what happened to it.

At this point in the working drawings, I had a full enough understanding of the house to design the lighting. Although an electrical contractor could lay out a system according to code, an architect wants much more. Proper lighting enhances the architectural space, lights various tasks according to their needs, and allows for changes in mood. It is so important that an architect could take a whole course in nothing but lighting—and still have a lot to learn from experience.

The kinds of lighting I use in a house vary. At Wind Whistle I relied in some places on movable floor or table lamps, in others (such as kitchen counters) on permanent direct lighting. Throughout the house I provided what architects call "ambient" lighting, which means the light that allows someone to use a room comfortably, to walk around or to sit and talk.

Each room had different requirements. For ambient lighting I used simple bulb holders on a light track, with the light aimed at the ceiling. (No one wants to look right at the source of light.) These lights are on dimmer switches so we can easily control the amount of light in a room. When we have a candlelight supper, the light is just enough to let us see what we are eating; when I am up early on a winter morning, the light can be strong to read a newspaper.

Finding just the right fixtures for a hall light and for a bathroom light was surprisingly difficult. Because lighting is so important, I consider these fixtures part of design development rather than finishing touches. The wrong fixture can be an awkward or jarring feature in a room rather than a decorative addition. I did not want anything formal, clichéd, or ordinary: no brass coach lights, cut-crystal chandeliers, or plain globes. At the Merchandise Mart in Chicago, where we looked for an occasional chair, I located two fixtures both Susan and I liked. One, in the hallway, has a geometric series of colored marbles set into its white glass shade. The other, in the bathroom, is a scalloped glass shell. Both are graceful, unassuming, but whimsical.

After I had finished the lighting layout, I still had to write the specifications, a description of certain elements required for the house. For Wind Whistle, I needed only three pages, but my words had to be absolutely precise. Writing these "specs" is not as much fun as drawing, but it does give me the satisfaction of an important job well done. Like every other part of the design process that precedes actual building, it takes time.

At last, however, I had completed my construction documents. With eight sets of these under my arm, I met Larry and Mark at the site, where we would "stake out" the house. I handed over my drawings and specs, gave some final instructions, and left for England with Susan—a sign of great confidence not only in our two builders but also in the documents. As our plane flew over the ocean, we both thought back to the site of Wind Whistle. Now, we knew with excitement, the construction process had begun.

THE CONSTRUCTION PROCESS

Construction of Wind Whistle began by staking out the house and setting the first-floor height. I had earlier walked over the site, eyeballed the height, and pounded some sticks into the ground. But this time everything was for real—and permanent. Larry Smith and Mark Vogen, our contractor/carpenters, arrived with the proper surveying equipment. Because no one can fully visualize the layout—the precise placement of the building in relation to trees, for example—until the house is measured on the ground, my documents always state: "The architect and owner must approve of the final location of the building on the site before construction begins." Since the architect *was* the owner at Wind Whistle, agreeing on the location was easy!

After staking out the house, indicating with stakes and string the basic plan or "footprint," Larry and Mark drove a large nail in a nearby tree to establish ground-floor height. This height is critical. At Wind Whistle, we had to be certain that roof and surface water drainage would flow properly in a natural direction toward the lake. It is not quite as easy to manage this flow as it may sound. The house forms a barrier to moving water. As anyone knows who has seen trees uprooted by a small stream, water is a mighty force. We had to be prepared for a heavy rainstorm when water could possibly rush over the threshold or through the middle of the house. If flowing water needs to be diverted, its diversion in turn may cause problems on the site, such as erosion, gullies, or standing water. For many homeowners, a familiar sign of poorly planned drainage is water in the basement.

Both Susan and I came to the staking-out. I urge my clients to be there, since many of them cannot really visualize how a house fits on a site from plans and a model. Participating in the staking also gives them a chance to be part of the process from its very beginning—rather like "bonding" with a newborn baby.

After gerrymandering the stakes to avoid major trees, we gave an okay to Mark, Larry, and Denny Hewitt, the excavator. When we left for our long-planned vacation in England, I worried because our house was located on a limestone bluff, and Denny had not been sure how deep the stone lay and whether he could handle it with his small bulldozer. If he couldn't, someone would have to be called in to blast it away, an expensive and time-consuming process. Two weeks later, in a remote corner of Dorset, snapshots arrived at our hotel. To my relief, we saw from the pictures that the excavation and trenches were neatly in place. (Trenches are the final dig, set precisely to take the footings, which are what the house sits on. Footings are a continuous band under the walls, made of wood or concrete, that spreads out the weight of the house so that it remains stable.)

I was excited by the pictures, because even after all my experience, I still find it magical to see drawings begin to take a physical shape. I could look at the holes and trenches and imagine a house. Susan, who tried to share my excitement (she saw only holes), was more pleased by an accompanying watercolor sketch, done by Jim Foran. He had drawn the house for her as a birthday present. At the bottom of the watercolor was a lovely green rattlesnake, waving its tail cheerily in the air. Jim knew that Susan fretted about having rattlesnakes as neighbors. His snake looked quite friendly.

When we returned home after three weeks, the wood foundation sat securely on top of the footings. Although concrete footings and foundation are more common, I prefer to use treated wood for both, since it is impervious to deterioration when properly installed, easy to insulate, and doesn't need cold-weather protection. Concrete, or the mortar used with concrete blocks, can't be exposed to freezing weather while it cures, which usually takes several days. ("Curing" is the chemical reaction that causes the mixture to turn from soup to solid.) Since the same carpenters who are working on the rest of the house can install the wood foundation, it goes up faster too.

At Wind Whistle I specified a continuous bed of gravel, about ten inches deep and two feet wide, to be laid underneath the 2×10-inch treated footings to promote good drainage. Studs (2×8-inch treated construction-grade wood used to build the frame of the house) are nailed on top of the footings. This is the basic structure of the house upon which everything else is built. (The horizontal boards that will support the floor are called "joists," as are construction boards, sloped or flat, that form the roof framing (also called "rafters"). In general, joists are horizontal; studs are vertical. This terminology is fundamental in understanding a contractor or carpenter.

At this stage of construction, the site is a mess. Dirt is heaped in piles and a big stack of lumber sits on one side. After the floor framing was done, strengthening the walls, Denny would return with his earth-moving equipment to level out the dirt and put the site more in order.

The first part of the framing went fast, as it usually does. About once a week, Susan came down with me to the site. In the beginning she was very eager to see the progress Larry and Mark had made. "Oh, wow! Here's the living room! There's the dining room! I can see now how the bedroom goes!" she exclaimed as the walls went up. At this stage the wood looks and smells fresh, sawdust curls in corners, and everyone has a general sensation of speed. By July, Susan had begun to plan our Thanksgiving dinner at Wind Whistle.

But I have watched lots of houses going up. I told her not to order a turkey yet. As construction continues, it moves more slowly. The rough plumbing has to be installed ("rough" means all the pipes that will be hidden in the walls). So does the rough electrical work, providing all the current to outlets and fixtures. If ductwork for heating and cooling is required, it has to go in. Water service and a sewer system have to be put in place. In a rural area like ours, this means a well and a septic tank with drainfield (the underground bed of porous gravel or rock that disseminates waste liquids); in a town or city, the house will be tied into water and sewer mains in the street.

None of this work, though essential, is very thrilling to watch in progress. It is hard to ooh and ah over pipes and tilework, and the only sign of progress after the workers installed our septic tank was a devastated piece of ground. (Since all the small trees and shrubs had been torn out of the soil, we decided to seed the surrounding drainfield and make a kind of meadow.)

When the carpenters begin on interior finishing, building seems to slow to a crawl. Sheetrock, plaster, wood walls, and tile all require careful fitting and hand labor. Outside, the roof has to be shingled. The exterior finish material has to be applied to walls and doors, which in turn will often have to be painted or stained. Exterior railings, decks, and other outdoor work have to be completed. Then interior millwork is installed: cabinets, doors, bookshelves, and other built-ins.

At this point in construction, many, many weeks have passed. Like many first-time clients, Susan became discouraged. "Why can't Larry and Mark just hire more help?" she asked plaintively. I've heard that query from other impatient owners, and I always have to explain that the solution isn't quite so simple. Just as only so many cooks can hover over one stove, only a certain number of carpenters can work efficiently at one time. Perhaps more important, carpenters would have a bleak and uncertain life if they had to spend much of their time waiting around for work to begin. Few areas of the country—and western Wisconsin is no exception—have a pool of skilled workers available at a moment's notice.

Sometimes scheduling doesn't work; the plumbers, a contractor tells an owner, have to finish up so-and-so's house and can't appear for a new job until late next week. The Sheetrock goes up only after the rough plumbing, electrical, and heating installations are finished, so work grinds to a near-halt. At Wind Whistle, one of our carpenters took his usual and well-earned two-week vacation in August. Susan alternately fussed and thought of other things, and Thanksgiving came and went, then Christmas. When spring arrived, the pace picked up. Grant Frerichs, our painter, arrived to apply the interior stains, paint, and miscellaneous finishes. Paul Steiner, our plumber/electrician, fit all the plumbing and electrical fixtures. More painting and finishing. Grant hung the wallpaper. Arne Johnson tiled the bathroom. Pete Wagner laid the wood floors and built some cabinets. Grant finished and sealed the floors. Every stage involved what seemed to Susan like endless delays. But finally, soon after Easter, we moved in.

I have named most of our major workers on the house because they are the ones who built it. If I added the names of their assistants, the list would be even longer. During our trip to England while Wind Whistle was going up, Susan and I spent one afternoon in the crumbling but still beautiful Italianate garden of a Tudor country house called Mapperton. The garden, with its terraces, summerhouses, fish ponds, and enclosing walls, was laid out in the 1920s. Affixed to one wall was a simple bronze plaque listing the names and trades of those who created the garden: "G. Symes, Builder; C. Dawe, Mason; G. Bacon, Labourer," until the last of eleven, "Also Colonel Lloyd." All, it stated, "Carried Out the Work of Making This Garden." It gave credit where credit was due. I hope I have done the same.

Even I had underestimated the time needed for construction, but that was because it involved some necessary complications. Since the cliff side of the house stands high off the ground, outside work was difficult. One false move, and good-bye whoever. Just once—but it was unforgettable—I saw a carpenter fall off the roof of a house I had under construction. He survived, but he was badly hurt. Larry, Mark, and Grant were reasonably cautious, they had great agility, and they avoided accidents. But they couldn't race along the high ridges of the roof. Their work on that side took time.

Although the framing looked straightforward on paper, the octagonal plan and the many different roof shapes meant that Larry and Mark had to do a great deal of careful fitting. They are marvelous old-fashioned craftsmen, and they are nothing if not careful. Sometimes I wanted to blurt out, "It's okay, be sloppy! Save a few hundred hours! After all, most of your work will be covered up anyway." But I didn't, and I'm glad. In the long run, good work pays off, whether it is visible or not. Now, after three years at Wind Whistle, not a crack shows.

Larry's and Mark's skills managed certain construction details that I couldn't visualize on drawings. As I mentioned in Chapter 13 when I discussed drawing up the plans, I try not to put more on the drawings than I know. I show the desired effect, but not always the way to achieve it. Larry and Mark knew when to ask questions and when to simply do what came naturally. For example, I could not figure out exactly how the overhangs would come together at an intersection. I could see that they formed a logical connection, but I couldn't describe how to make it. Larry and Mark just went ahead and fitted them out, perfectly. When they confronted the roof over Jenny's room, which has an unusual curve to it, they weren't sure how to shingle it properly. They asked me, I worked out the geometry, and we found a solution together.

One pleasing detail in the living area is the result of Larry's and Mark's ingenuity. When I drew a rounded enclosure for the stairwell, I specified that it be covered with wood boards and assumed they would have to be vertical to conform to the curve, I wished they could run horizontally, like the other wood boards in the house, but I couldn't see how that could be done. By making deep saw cuts every ⅜ inch on the back of the boards, Mark and Larry were able to bend the boards without breaking them. The eye-catching curve of seemingly solid wood makes many visitors pause to admire it.

Just as I did not interfere with their decisions about how best to approach their work, they did not usurp my responsibilities and decisions about design. Clear separation of roles can sometimes be awkward with a contractor who is used to "design/build"—to planning a house as well as building it. At the same time we were working on Wind Whistle, I was supervising a small summerhouse in western Minnesota. Its builder, a first-rate contractor and a wonderful man, had done almost all his work in this small town as design/build. So he kept trying to be helpful, making suggestions to the owners. "This railing detail is awfully plain," he'd say to them. "I have a really cute railing I built on the Olsons' house. Why don't you drive over tonight and take a look at it?" Or "If you want, we could just continue this curving floor out at the end and have a cute little balcony." The owners, who were great clients, always called me up. They knew that "cute" is not my favorite word. I valued the contractor's enthusiasm. But finally, I took the plunge and said firmly, "Tell Harris to *build*. I will design!" He got the point, and we stayed friends.

The construction process is a fairly predictable one, but it does usually involve certain changes. However careful and detailed the plans are, they need some adjustment as the house goes up. Almost to the very day when Larry and Mark were going to start building it, I continued to change the size and shape of our deck. Everyone had an opinion. Susan wanted a huge deck, where she envisioned herself lying in a large hammock. (I hate metal hammock stands, which are ugly, and I don't much like lying in hammocks, either.) Although I pointed out that the western exposure of the deck would often make it too hot for lounging, she wasn't convinced. Larry rather liked the idea of a multilevel deck that stepped down, perhaps to a barbecue platform. When the house was framed up, I could stand at floor level and look around. I could then locate the treetops precisely and see that my initial triangular shape did not work. I was determined to have the deck "float" among the trees, not cut the trees to accommodate the deck. My final plan, which is simple in plan and fairly small, works fine. Susan, who never gives up, has ordered a hanging hammock for the garden house.

The tiny deck just off our bedroom required another modification. I had initially designed several possible shapes that jutted out at an angle. During construction, I realized that the simplest and most elegant solution was to "square off" the bedroom floor into a logical corner, forming the outside balcony.

An on-site architect can often see ingenious ways to make the best of an awkward situation. When the plumber had installed the hot-water heater and holding tank in our bathroom, I realized that they were more obtrusive than I had expected. So I had the carpenters hide them behind a partial wall. After the wall was stained an attractive rosy pink, it became an ideal spot to hang towel bars.

The geometry of the upstairs study forced another handy adaptation. Because of its shape, the inner wall of the downstairs master bedroom had two large alcoves, starting at about seven feet above the floor, too high to reach. We pondered quite a bit about how to use them. "A storage area?" "No, too hard to get to." "A place for sculpture?" "No, that would just look funny." "A place for dust?" "That's for sure!" So we ended up placing a recessed light in each, with dimmers, bouncing beams off the ceiling. It was a perfect solution for the bedroom lighting.

One last-minute change that failed to improve the original design was a seemingly minor one. I decided to eliminate a small storage room near the front door in order to provide covered outdoor wood storage. Somehow I'd forgotten Susan's need to stockpile lots of "extras"—extra paper towels, extra tuna fish, extra cereal. (I'll admit her forethought does often come in handy. She reminds me of this whenever I call for another roll of toilet paper.) After moving in, we soon found we needed more storage. Fortunately, the crawl space under our dining area turned out to have more headroom than I'd expected, so we finished it off for storage that would be accessible from outdoors, below the deck. That helped, as did Larry's suggestion to build shelves in the empty space beneath the curving stairwell. That space has become an invaluable kitchen pantry.

Some of the decisions an architect has to make during construction are aesthetic as well as practical, such as how a building meets the ground. Where does the wood siding stop and the foundation begin? What material should be applied between the ground line and the finished siding? At Wind Whistle, I had drawn neat straight lines, following the slope of the land, but in practice they didn't work out neat *or* straight. I made adjustments and proposed aluminum flashing for the "in-between" space. Now I am slowly adding wild tiger lilies around the base of the house to soften the line between flashing and ground.

One surprise was our dining-room table. Susan and I had made several forays into furniture stores and design emporia, and we couldn't find a dining table we liked. So, well into construction, I designed a stone table, with a top 2½ inches thick and a sturdy steel base. Its shape reflected the shape of the room. Since I had no experience with stone, I had not realized just how heavy this table would be. When delivery came, I learned quickly. The top weighed 900 pounds, and it arrived in three pieces, each of which required four of us to carry. I was amazed at how skillfully the stone craftsmen doweled these pieces together into a single handsome (and absolutely immovable) 4×8-foot top. Where the dining table stands now, it will always stand

The uneasiest moments for me during the construction process were probably when Susan and I drove down to inspect the interior wood stains and, later, the exterior paint. Although we had done a number of color studies during the design phase and had tested the stains on samples of board, color often has a completely different impact on walls than it does on a small sample or a color chip. I have always leaned toward natural wood finishes ("Leave that beautiful woodwork as it is!"), and I was very uncertain about tinted stains. But Susan, my client, loves color, and I planned for her to have it.

On the interior wood, mainly ceilings and stairwell, I wanted the grain to show through the color and to give the "feel" of wood. With the wise advice of our paint consultant, we diluted the stain, applied it, and then wiped off the residue to reveal the wood, yet leave vivid color. A clear varnish preserved the color from fingerprints, fly residue, and airborne pollutants like smoke. This all sounded foolproof, yet the night before we were to drive to Wind Whistle to see the newly stained blue ceiling in the living room, I tossed and turned. What if the color was muddy? What if it was too dark? Too light? What if I just plain didn't like it? Or Susan didn't like it? "There's nothing we can do," I told her gloomily. "Once it's stained, it's stained. Let's hope for the best."

The best, thank heavens, was what we got. Seeing how attractive the sky-blue ceiling looked, I was encouraged to order stain in different colors for the other rooms. When we came to the point of picking exterior colors, however, I got cold feet again. I had never designed a painted house before. Larry, who also loves natural wood, joined with me in trying to dissuade Susan from her adamant stand on color. "Look at this beautiful redwood siding," I urged her. "Do you really want to cover it up with paint?" She studied me coolly. I know that look. The night before *that* inspection trip, I tossed and turned more. A bright lemon yellow? Apple-green trim? No modernist architect would have rested easy.

But, after an initial eye-blinking reaction, I soon came to love the bright colors. So did Susan. With Grant, our painter, now in collusion, she asked for and got rosy-red and lavender touches on other parts of the trim. I liked them all. By the time I designed our garden house two years later, it was quite natural for me to dream up a rainbow-hued roof. I am still fond of unpainted wood (below its colored roof, the garden house has a siding of plain cedar shingles), but I have been converted to a much wider, bolder, and even somewhat humorous palette. Of all our decisions on the house during the construction process, the one to use lots of color has probably given us both the most pleasure.

Did anything go seriously wrong during the construction process? Fortunately, no. I had many years of experience in building houses, and my contractors, Larry and Mark, were men of skill, honesty, and enthusiasm. We made a good team. Did the house cost more than I'd thought it would? Yes, about 20 percent more, but I was aware of each decision I made that led to that figure. As I have explained earlier, I foresaw possible complications, and I was able to absorb the extra costs. I had deliberately chosen to work from an estimate on a "cost-plus" basis, a procedure I do not always advise for my clients, and I kept a close eye on procedures. A valued and repeat client of mine told me when I designed his first house, "Pretend you are spending your own money." I have kept that advice in mind, and I never specify anything without an acute awareness of its cost.

When the house was finished, the last step in the construction process was to clean up. Larry and Mark removed the pile of scrap lumber I'd told them to save for the wood stove; it held too much wood of too many sizes mixed in with junk. Our wild acreage had plenty of kindling, and besides, I decided, we were tired of construction mess. As good contractors should, Larry and Mark left a clean site. For the first time in ten months, we could walk around our house without watching our feet. We had finished grades where they were supposed to be. Now we could start landscaping. Out came Susan's garden catalogs, and we began to plan our finishing touches.

FINISHING
TOUCHES

When a contractor carts away a last load of debris and an architect receives a last payment, a house is technically finished. But work still remains. I call this work "finishing touches," although it is much more important than the quick light brushwork that "touch" implies. The most important tasks left for the homeowner to tackle, either alone or with expert help, are landscaping and interior decoration.

Both landscaping and interior decoration involve design, but they do not necessarily involve the architect. Yet since my clients know that I care passionately about their (*our*) houses, many of them do ask my advice. In a recently built house, for example, my clients wanted an all-white interior, and they asked me to help them select the right white from the hundreds of available hues. It was a crucial decision, and together we found the perfect shade.

But I do not consider myself qualified to complete an entire interior with fabrics, furniture, color, and artwork. Although that is what I have quite happily done in each of my own five houses, I do not want to impose my personality on my clients' interior decorating. They usually seek advice from many sources, often including interior designers, and all my clients have done a remarkable job. I like to think that they picked me as their architect because they have good taste!

Similarly, although I consider the house in its environment very carefully, I am not qualified as a landscape architect, and I do not try to plan the grounds around my clients' houses, nor do I order specific plantings. I strongly suggest that my clients retain a landscape architect, and I often recommend one to them. Local nurseries do provide landscaping service, but their designs are usually neither sophisticated nor special enough for an individually designed modernist house.

At Wind Whistle, landscaping presented an immediate problem. After clearing shrubs and trees for the drainfield of the septic system, we were faced with a sweep of bare dirt on the land side of the house. Below the deck, construction had left a steep pitch of raw clay. In the wooded area bordered by the driveway, we had had to remove over forty dead or dying elm trees, and the tree-cutting equipment had chewed up another large area. Everywhere we looked that spring, we saw clay, mud, and uprooted plants.

I realized that we were going to need some serious and careful landscape design. This had not been part of my original concept for Wind Whistle; cabins in wild areas often do not require much landscape planning. At our family cabin in northern Wisconsin, for example, I had designed the structure to sit in the midst of the woods. We had no lawn, no plantings, no garden, no upkeep. Clearly Wind Whistle was going to be different.

Another important consideration was Susan's desire for a garden. When she saw the sunny spaces left by all the construction and clearing, she no longer thought of mud and clay—but of phlox, daylilies, delphiniums, and shrub roses. At our city house in Minneapolis, we had only a tiny garden, and most of it was in the shade. She reminded me of the large (though usually weedy) garden she'd left at her old house when we married. She was tired of impatiens and begonias, she said wistfully, and as she walked around the bare patches of earth that now surrounded Wind Whistle, her eyes gleamed.

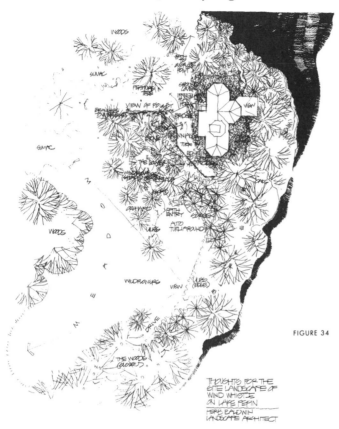

FIGURE 34

So I retained Herb Baldwin, an experienced landscape architect, to come to our site, walk around it, take away the floor plans and site plan, and suggest a design. He produced a rough sketch from which we worked, with gradual additions and some changes. This procedure is not standard for most landscape designers, who prefer to supply "full service," with finished sketches, consultations, and suggestions for specific plantings that they can arrange and oversee. But Herb and I have worked together for a long time, and I knew he had a quick eye and unusual creativity. He knew that I was somewhat over-budget on the house and that I did not want a formal plan. So he made one visit, a plan, several sketches, and a great contribution to Wind Whistle.

A landscape architect has the ability to look at a site and think in curves, angles, and all kinds of geometric forms, while considering color, height, texture and other variables. It is rather like an architect's ability to imagine the whole of a house and its individual rooms at the same time. For Wind Whistle, Herb located an approach to the front door that wound through a small glade, creating in its gentle turns a sense of suspense and in its wooded overhang a sense of a fairy-tale transition to a magical cottage. He suggested a simple terraced garden just outside the front door, bisected by the entry path, and a short wooden bridge over a small gully that would otherwise make the path uncomfortably wet at certain times of the year (Figure 34).

To implement his plan, we called in Julie Peterson, an experienced "plantswoman" from a nursery in nearby Red Wing. Julie helped us plan how to treat the large devastated area left by the removal of all the dead trees, and she had it seeded into a grassy meadow with scattered fruit trees. With permission from the developer of the bluff on which we'd built, we arranged to move eight large pine trees from one of his nearby plantations so that they would screen the house from view and line the driveway. Finally, Julie plotted out the garden, brought in railroad ties and lots of dirt, and gave Susan a tempting empty canvas to fill with plants of her choice. As her own "finishing touch," Julie found us a marvelously twisted small pine tree to sit by the front door. It has a unique shape, idiosyncratic as the house itself.

Nothing has given us quite as much surprising pleasure at Wind Whistle as our garden. From early spring to late fall, Susan reads mail-order nursery catalogs with the same engrossed attention she gives to a new novel or memoir. Bit by bit, the garden has expanded, as she comes home from a visit to a nursery with yet another "find," perhaps a plant she's never grown before or an old favorite that happened to be on sale. Although she tends to stick plants here and there quite casually, and the garden has no formal plan, it is a beautiful tangle of color from the early-spring daffodils and tulips through the lush flowers of mid-summer. As part of our life at Wind Whistle, we take regular "garden tours" in the early morning and after dinner. With a cup of coffee or a glass of wine, we stroll together around the borders. As Susan points out each day's new bloom, we get just as excited by one daylily that has flowered for the first time as we do by a grand English garden. Susan's garden is clearly one "finishing touch" that will probably never end.

As the garden took on increasing importance in Susan's life, I gradually realized that Wind Whistle needed one more addition, a small garden house. This is the kind of finishing touch that often occurs to an owner a year or two, or more, after moving in. For us, it took two years of acquiring garden tools, from spades to clippers, which began to stack up outside our door and tumble down over our toes. Our front steps overflowed with buckets, pots, bags of peat moss and cattle manure, bottles of fertilizer, spray bottles, rubber boots, and other items that mysteriously appeared in regular packages from UPS. We needed some place to store all this stuff. (You'll remember my earlier assertions about Putting Stuff Somewhere It Won't Show.)

We also had found that our unshaded deck on the bluff side of the house, with its fantastic view of the Mississippi, was too hot during most summer days for a comfortable outdoor lunch or even for late-morning coffee. We began to talk of a little screened porch somewhere nearby in the shade, "when we can afford it." Susan claims that being brought up in Iowa gives her more budgetary sense than I have, and it is true that I usually decide I don't want to wait until I'm really old (or dead) to enjoy a tempting trip, a superb meal—or a combined screened porch and garden house.

Since Susan had a landmark birthday, her fiftieth, approaching, I decided to surprise her with a Lake Pepin "folly." Besides, she could hardly argue we couldn't afford it when it was already built. We were flying to England to tour gardens in mid-May; we'd be gone from Wind Whistle for almost two weeks; her birthday was in June. I could have it built while we were gone. After consultation with my friendly banker in nearby Maiden Rock, Wisconsin, I began to plan.

A garden house presented me with the kind of design challenge I enjoy. Although it had to relate aesthetically to the house, it could have a special feeling all its own. In the past few years, I have had the chance to design several such structures, ranging from a simple free-standing screened porch to an elaborate outdoor room complete with television and sauna. I'm never quite sure what to call them. "Out-building" sounds rather like either an outdoor privy or perhaps a mail-order prefabricated toolshed or the kind of miniature barn sold in lumberyards. "Gazebo" is a little fancy, and "folly" is a British word that can sound odd when transplanted to a Midwestern landscape.

Since I've been given complete freedom to design these small out-door structures, I've felt the same kind of exhilaration beginning each plan as I do taking the first ski run down six inches of new powder. They provide me both great fun and an absorbing challenge. Just because they are lighthearted and small doesn't mean they are frivolous designs, tossed off in a few hours' work. This kind of outdoor structure has to satisfy functional requirements in a small amount of space, be easy to maintain, and yet stand up to high winds and bad storms over a long period of time.

At Wind Whistle, I had to be very particular about where to locate the garden house. The obvious spot was in the small glade through which our wood-chip path led to the main house. The glade was close enough so we could easily carry meals on a tray back and forth, and it was shaded and sited toward the wild part of the property. If I miscalculated, however, our carpenters would have to remove so many trees in the glade that we would no longer have enough shade. I also wanted the screened porch to have at least a partial view of the garden when it was in flower and a view of the absolutely untouched woods as a contrast.

The structure as I finally placed it (Figure 35) wraps around a handsome though smallish chestnut tree on one side and skirts a stand of

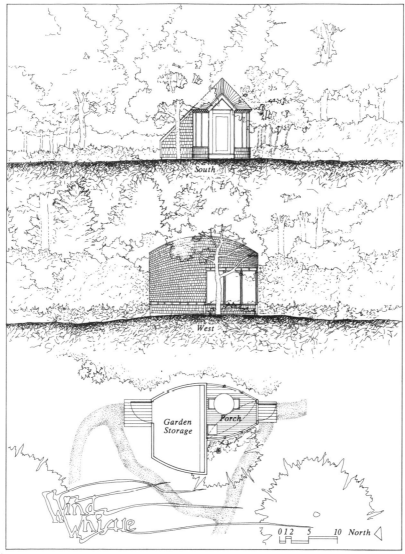

FIGURE 35

spindly hawthorns on the other. These are "scrub" trees, almost like bushes, easily pulled out. I took the precaution of having them tied back, out of the way of workmen, while construction was going on. These spindly trees might seem incidental, even unattractive from the perspective of a formal planting. But they shelter and partially shade the garden house, and as we sit in the screened porch, we feel we are in a very different environment from our main house. It seems, we both agree, as if we are back at summer camp, with the kind of appealing but haphazard setting that most camp buildings have.

As part of my planning, I set the building on a wooden platform just above the ground rather than on a concrete slab. This meant that the root system of the trees would be undisturbed, and they would be naturally watered as before. This is an example of a technical decision, disturbing the existing natural environment as little as possible, that influenced design—all to the good.

An outbuilding like ours, which combines a storage shed and screened porch, can take virtually any shape. My design looks something like an upside-down boat, a form that took its inspiration primarily from Jenny's curving bedroom ceiling in the main house, but also from an outdoor pavilion in western Minnesota I'd recently designed (see Chapter 3, "When an Architect and Client Sit Down to Work"). Architects often go through periods of working with certain shapes and styles, and I have lately been intrigued by the proportions, shifting shadows, and spacious feeling of this curvilinear, vaulted form.

At one end of the structure is the shed, with room to hold a riding lawn mower, bicycles, and garden equipment, as well as miscellaneous storage (like Susan's cache of extra toilet paper). By dividing the interior space with a seven-foot-high wall that extends upward only to the beginning of the curving roof shape, I separated the two halves of the garden house visually, yet I kept the high roof visible from both sides. If I had extended the wall all the way up to the roof, which would be the usual way of dividing one large room, we would have lost the impression of soaring space. Standing in the shed, we now look up toward the vaulting ceiling; in the screened porch on the other end, we enjoy the same perspective.

Although I wanted Susan to choose the interior trim colors for the garden house, I devised an exterior roof of prestained cedar shingles, in alternating rows reflecting six of the seven colors of the rainbow (red, orange, yellow, green, blue, violet). This "rainbow roof" was a tribute to Susan's affection for vibrant color, and it was a kind of musical variation on the color themes of the main house.

After we arrived home from England to an almost completed garden house, we found—as always happens with any structure—that we wanted some finishing touches on our "finishing touch"! Susan encouraged me to stain the interior ceiling green, much as we'd stained interior wood in the main house, to continue the feeling of the green trees and grass around the building. We added some functional hardware on the shed door, painted some exterior trim in green, lavender, and red, and purchased four different colors of canvas deck chairs for the porch. As a sort of grace note, Susan found a multicolored cotton hammock that just fit (barely) when suspended crosswise from two corner posts (not, thank heavens, from an ugly metal frame.) After our experiments with bold color in Wind Whistle, we charged ahead confidently on this smaller project.

We also had fun with our interior decorating at Wind Whistle. Not all of my clients enjoy this part of "finishing touches" as much as we did, and with good reason. It can be enormously time-consuming, especially with a large house to decorate. It can also cause arguments. Fortunately, Susan and I had already worked together on the addition I'd built to my house when we married, and we knew each other's tastes. Perhaps more important, we knew we had something to learn from each other.

When I first met Susan, I was taken aback by her style of decorating her own house. It was eclectic, riotously colorful, and (to my eye) rather crowded. Everywhere I turned in her small rooms, I had to dodge a mobile or a hanging plant. As she proudly pointed out to me, her decorating was also done "on the cheap." (Professors make even less money than architects.) Her stair carpeting, for example, was unforgettable: a sort of hot orange, which had evidently been an equally hot bargain in the remnant corner of a local discount carpet emporium. When she saw my house, she liked its style and simplicity, but she thought it seemed rather bare and somewhat cold. She brought color and liveliness to my taste, and I brought restraint and discipline to hers. (She doesn't see it quite that way, and she once wrote a very funny but pointed essay called "Living with an Architect." I have to admit it brought her grateful letters from several other wives of architects!)

Our choices in furniture were fairly easy, although we had to look for a while to find just what we wanted and could afford (as most clients do). Since we immediately agreed that we were not furnishing a typical cabin, we definitely did not want country pine, braided rugs, or hearth brooms. Nor did we want chrome, brown leather, or white linen. Instead we looked for contemporary pieces that were simple, elegant, very comfortable, and colorful.

Two exceptions were what Susan calls "finds" from Minneapolis junk stores, places I have to be dragged into but Susan loves (she calls them "antique shops"). I was surprised to hear myself agreeing that a small carved chaise longue, probably from the 1920s, was just the right scale for Susan's study. I'm sure she liked the idea of reading or correcting manuscripts while lounging on this little sofa like the Empress Josephine. Its curving lines are quite graceful, and it adds a feminine touch to the sleek and functional surfaces of the study. We also found an inexpensive old oak cabinet that just fit into a corner of the living room, providing show-off storage for Susan's vases and assorted doodads.

Our shopping was not difficult, partly because we had some excellent resources. Although we did some browsing on a trip to New York, we found our sofas in Minneapolis at a store that specializes in international design. On another trip, this time to Chicago, we located the right occasional chair at the Merchandise Mart, and I ordered our unobtrusive but distinctive reading lamps from a catalog. (I do not tell my clients to go to New York and Chicago to furnish their houses; we happened to have other reasons for our travels. But having access to a large metropolitan area, and/or to a decorator, and/or to catalogs, helps.)

Since we could not find the right coffee table, I designed one. Its octagonal glass top sits on Mankato Kasota stone slabs, the same stone used in the tops of the dining-room and deck tables. A typical finishing touch was Susan's idea of cutting dark blue and red felt squares to fit on top of the slabs, so the color would show through the glass. I also designed our bedside tables and bedframes, which were painted in yellow and pink to match the wallpaper, as well as a bedroom cabinet, which was stained blue like the ceiling. Since I knew Susan would want lots of books around, I had arranged built-in oak shelves throughout the house.

The part of decorating Susan liked best was choosing Oriental rugs. We had decided to add color, pattern, and warmth to the oak floors with one or two; we ended up with six. In her own houses, Susan had always used rather weird area rugs, either from carpet-remnant clearances or from garage or tag sales. On her first visit to my house, she fell in love with a large Persian rug (with me, too, she assures me), and it was the one piece of my furnishings she did not want to change after we were married. We looked at lots of Orientals for Wind Whistle, took some home on approval (and took many back), and learned what we could about their types, styles, and history. Once Susan had recovered from "sticker shock," she began to think of Orientals as an investment in lasting beauty. Before long, her bargain instinct surfaced, and she began to haggle enthusiastically with the willing salesperson.

Each salesperson convinced her that she had chosen just the very rug he had hoped to buy for himself, an irreplaceable gem that he had let her have at a price liable to bankrupt him. On the way home from these expeditions, I would tease her about how merciless she was. "How could you ruin Ali's day like that? How can you live with yourself after you've deprived him of the very rug he'd been saving for himself?" When we had completed our furnishings for

Wind Whistle, Susan said her only regret was that she had no more excuses to tootle around the Twin Cities examining Oriental rugs.

Most of our finishing touches were not that costly. On our walls we hung inexpensive and often whimsical prints, etchings, and posters. Two of our favorites are framed sheets of English wrapping paper, illustrations from *The Church Mice Chronicles*, a brilliant series of children's books by English author Graham Oakley. One decorating trick I learned long ago was to take apart a book of well-produced prints, like Georgia O'Keeffe's flowers, frame each page in an inexpensive Lucite box, and mass them together for maximum effect. We used this technique in several places at Wind Whistle, sometimes with calendars or unusual greeting cards whose attractive graphics had caught our attention.

Although we had not thought we'd need window coverings in such a private setting, we soon discovered that the bright western sun pouring through southern and western windows heated our rooms too quickly in summer. We also thought it might be useful to close the windows from viewing in our absence, since curious sightseers, noticing the construction activity from the road far below, sometimes managed to find their way through a labyrinth of dirt roads to our door. So we added further color with narrow metal horizontal blinds for the windows and vertical fabric blinds for the two sliding doors.

Each of these decisions involved shopping, comparison, consultation, and checking samples or pieces on approval. As I tell my clients, it takes lots of time to finish a house properly, and they should not push themselves to do it in a hurry. If they do, they'll not only fail to enjoy the process at all, but they may make mistakes they'll regret later. Months after we'd moved in, we were still adding a little here, a little there—a striking multicolored wind flag for the deck, a sunshade for the deck table, a Chinese umbrella stand to hold our small collection of English walking sticks.

This kind of interior decoration can be pleasurable, and most clients enjoy at least some of it, provided they have both time and money to spend. What they may forget is the energy also required for the final nitty-gritty details of furnishing a house, the sorts of tasks home-decorating magazines seldom mention. On many mornings Susan, who prides herself on organization, determinedly clutched a long scribbled list as she left our Minneapolis house for Target or K-Mart. "I glaze over after about twenty minutes in there," she has told me, "so I have to move fast to get everything on the list." She returned laden with towel racks, dish drainer, silverware dividers, potholders, glassware, pots and pans, spatulas, knives, dishtowels, dishrags, clothes hangers, laundry basket, and enough more to fill the car on several trips to Wind Whistle. Someone has to take care of the household trivia, and Susan seems to enjoy it, although she will never admit it. In turn, I dutifully screw in the toilet-paper holder, fasten the towel racks, and hang the pictures. All this takes many hours (not to mention frustrating trips to the hardware store for missing screws, the right size of screwdriver, picture hangers, and so on.) Nobody moves into a new house on the day the carpenters leave and lies down on the sofa to read a good book.

But the day does eventually come when the last finishing touch is done—or *almost* the last finishing touch. As I've mentioned before, a house continues to evolve, sometimes in small but important ways, and sometimes in larger changes or additions, like our garden house. But an owner does reach a satisfactory level of completion, and it feels wonderful. These days as I deal out a hand of our lifetime gin rummy game after a long, lazy lunch on our deck, we look around us with a sense of gratitude and contentment. Wind Whistle is exactly as we want it. Of course, if Susan would only agree, there is just enough room on the end of the lot for a tiny one-room guest cottage . . .

CABIN FEVER: THE CLIENT'S FINAL REPORT

Sometimes when I am home in Minneapolis, perhaps writing at my desk, or pausing at my bedroom door to decide whether to water plants or fold laundry or pick up books from the floor, or dashing to the ringing phone, I think of Wind Whistle. I picture it, empty and silent, sunlight pouring through the large windows onto the wood floor. I let my mind walk slowly through its few rooms, noticing everything in place, swept and ready. Fresh wood lies by the stove, a clean towel hangs in the kitchen, a few magazines are neatly stacked on a low table. On the sofa is a small red cushion, plumped where I can put my head as I read. The house, I know, is waiting for me. Outside I can almost hear the wind whistling over the high-pitched roof and circling around the corners of the quiet bedroom.

Now that our house is finished, I find that I am more than a "satisfied client." I am a passionate partisan, devoted to Wind Whistle in ways that have caused me to change my life. Like many other Minnesotans I know, I now have "cabin fever." This is not winter claustrophobia, but an intense longing to escape to a special place of one's own. It is so powerful it can feel like missing an absent lover. When travel or unavoidable obligations have kept me away too long, I get itchy and irritable. I start crossing off items on my calendar with fierce determination; no party, concert, or meeting, I tell my husband with a fiery look in my eye, will keep me in town one more week.

I suppose I cannot really call Wind Whistle a cabin, since I could comfortably live there all year. Though Wind Whistle is not large, marble, or magnificent, I call it my Taj Mahal, because James created it with such exuberance and love. Fortunately, unlike the Indian mogul's wife, I am still alive to enjoy it. It has become more than a house. It is now a destination.

But the fact that Wind Whistle is definitely a house causes me some uneasiness. We do already have a house, a fairly new and pleasant one in Minneapolis. Not long ago, I read an interview with a local social activist, whose protests in good causes I have long admired. She was quoted as saying that although her husband wanted to build a vacation house on some land they owned in another state, she wouldn't hear of it. It seemed wrong, she said, in a world where many people are homeless, to have two houses.

Drawn to many varieties of guilt, I tried this one on for size. It seemed, uncomfortably, to fit. So then I wondered if I would feel better if Wind Whistle were just a log cabin, with no running water, maybe not even a pump outside the door. Would that also be a moral affront? What about a cabin with a sink but no toilet? Or a toilet, but no bathtub? If electric baseboards were not acceptable, was an old wood stove?

I often puzzle aloud with friends who, like me, are at the moment securely anchored in the middle class about the moral level of consumption acceptable for a socially responsible person. I have found that most people have an intuitive but very clear set of standards about what is all right and what is too much. Those standards are wildly variable, usually depending upon income. For one friend, a $30 sweater is okay, $50 is really stretching; for another, $75 doesn't seem unreasonable. Wandering through a local mall of exclusive shops, I can see women who find $200 not excessive. And, of course, unloading a contribution at the Free Store, which distributes clothing and household goods to the needy, I am aware that for many, budgets don't allow for any new sweater at all.

Once, during the construction of Wind Whistle, I asked a friend who lives in a large, elegant house whether, though she and her husband can afford it, she ever worried about its cost. "Well," she said thoughtfully, "suppose I insisted that our family give it up? Where do you think we should live? In a two-bedroom rambler outside the city? And why wouldn't *that* be too much? Should we give up a house entirely and move into a rented apartment? Instead of an apartment, why not a single room? Where do you decide to draw the line?"

I don't know. I haven't got answers for how other people ought to live. I do know that James and I are very fortunate to have a retreat. Wind Whistle means so much to me now that I cannot bear to think of giving it up. Like many Minnesotans, I talk about "getting away" to my cabin. We run from the hectic daily pace of our lives, the intrusive telephone and doorbell, domestic responsibilities.

What I notice first at Wind Whistle is the quiet. Although we do have a telephone, the concept of "long distance" inhibits most callers, and it absolutely eliminates the army of pollsters, charity solicitors, and salespeople for siding, insulation, light bulbs, and rug-cleaning services who regularly invade our house in the city. Although we have neighbors on the bluff, we seldom see them. All we hear is wind, thunder, rain, and sleet; an occasional train; and on summer nights, the rustlings and cracklings of mysterious small animals who prowl the woods just outside our windows.

This surrounding quiet cushions me. I lean back against it, slowly relaxing. At Wind Whistle I am able to unroll and stretch out, as if I were a thin piece of much-written-on parchment that has been bound too tightly too long and cannot easily lie flat. At Wind Whistle, I do lie flat—or curled up on the sofa. No one around me is working; my husband may sketch or make notes on a project, but he doesn't make me feel I need to get up and busy myself at my keyboard. When I want to write, I do. Otherwise I read, doze, play gin rummy with James, and look out the windows.

Most days, in all weather, I walk on the dusty, seldom-traveled roads and paths that connect our edge of the woods to the meadows and small farms beyond. On these walks, I find myself drifting into thoughts so light and wispy they usually get buried under the steamroller of burdened days. One early-winter morning in January at Wind Whistle, when the sun was warm and the wind almost balmy, I walked for an hour down a road that leads into some undeveloped lots in the woods. Hidden among the trees at the bluff's edge, I looked out on the frozen river through air so clear I could see the bends and curves of the opposite shoreline as if I were looking through an old-fashioned sharp-focused View-Master. High above, a bald eagle swept by, plunging and turning in the brilliant light that caught the white flash of its head and tail.

What I was thinking as I stood there I'm not sure. But suddenly two lines from an old-fashioned poem, the kind no one reads in school anymore, floated into my mind and hung there, like the eagle hovering far overhead: "A boy's will is the wind's will, / And the thoughts of youth are long, long thoughts." When I was old enough to think myself a scholar, but still too young to have developed much understanding, I scorned such poetry as sentimental and meaningless. Now I know why it has lasted. What I seldom seem to have time for, I said to myself, is exactly that: long, long thoughts. Thoughts that start nowhere in particular, meander along like a twisting country road, and pause at a wild rosebush or beside a trout stream covered with watercress. Thoughts that may not be deep, but are satisfyingly unbroken, flowing into one another like one of those streams.

In the distance, that morning on the bluff, I heard the faint whistle of a train. Trains run frequently on both sides of the river, chugging purposefully to and from Chicago with long strings of boxcars, but still singing the haunting song that used to draw me to the side of a track so I could watch the train flash by. Hearing a train whistle, I remember myself as a child, dreaming of strange cities, adventure, and romance.

The sound of that whistle, slowly fading into the distance, also gives me a sense of space. The train goes on and on, past Wind Whistle, along the river, across the plains. Listening, I track it in my mind. That is another gift of a retreat or cabin: reminders of a larger world. Confined in the city, we easily forget what lies out there. I often see only the relentless spread of houses, office buildings, and factories, and I picture "development" as an armored and unappeasable dragon, eating up more and more land, belching smoke into an already hazy sky. I imagine that no one dares to aim a dagger at its heart, for fear our economy would die along with the beast. So instead, many of us flee.

Speeding away from the city, beyond the encircling moats of freeways and scattered outposts of megamalls, I am always surprised how soon we are released into the country. As fields ripple past, like a softly shaken blanket outside our window, I begin to loosen as if I were being shaken too. My vision, unlocked from its narrow focus, zooms into the distance. Looking at the horizon, I am reminded how this sky sweeps north, over forests, past thousands of lakes, toward glacier and tundra. I also remember that not too far to the west, mountains break the flatness of the plains and march toward the Pacific. Following the Mississippi along the Wisconsin border, I am aware that this great river snakes its way to the Gulf.

Driving past the long views across the flatlands south of the Twin Cities, then turning to wind between the soft hills near Miesville and

New Trier, and finally passing beneath the bluffs of Red Wing, we see Wind Whistle in its larger setting. The journey not only reminds me of space, it gives me a gentle reprimand about time and mortality.

We do not make the mistake of thinking we own the land. Even as we plan and plant, I know that the small apple tree whose roots I heap with mulch against the drought, whose bark I tenderly wrap for the winter, whose dark lines I admire against the snow, may disappear into the woodland after I am gone. Here on the bluff, we are surrounded by evidence of earlier dwellers—Indian names, a broken fence around land gone wild, an abandoned and crumbling barn.

We also know we are city people, loving our bit of land but not belonging to it as those who work it do. At the end of our dead-end road is a well-kept, thriving farm. Its owners, now retired, have lived there for many years. The farmer still works a few fields, and in the fall his shocks of hay—old-fashioned bundles, almost antique in their effect —stand proudly in clean raked rows. His wife's flower garden and raspberry patch offer both color and bounty in the summer. Their bird-houses and birdbaths attract bluebirds to our road, and pheasants feed in their stubble. If anyone deserves to claim ownership of land, that couple does. As we drive to Wind Whistle, we recognize that in comparison, we are perched on our few acres like foreign birds who, migrating beyond their usual flyway, pause for a while before moving on.

Because I love the wild beauty of our land, I want it to remain unspoiled. That is one of the ironies of "cabin fever": no one wants anyone else to catch it. By building a house in the country, we are feeding the dragon. At Wind Whistle we have just the right number of neighbors. We are not anxious for more. And since we built near a path leading to a viewpoint, our neighbors may not have been delighted to see our house rise on once-vacant land.

A purist, who may well be right, would tell me that we should simply camp on our land, portaging in equipment, cleaning up after ourselves, and leaving no trace of our stay. But when I think of Wind

Whistle, waiting in silence for my next visit, I know how much I want a shell of my own. I move as comfortably inside it as if it were my own skin. Each detail of the house is a familiar friend, often with a history. I look upward toward the blue vaulted ceiling, watching a Japanese butterfly kite circle below the high painted beams, and I remember the day I found that kite in a museum shop. I think of the huge museum, the December weather outside, the noisy New York streets. I picture our master painter, Grant, carefully balancing on a tall ladder to hang the fragile silk kite.

I care intensely about what surrounds me indoors as well as out. Outdoors is wild and uncontrolled; I like to feel that inside is familiar and secure. When I open the door of our house, I am pleased that everything is in its place. I know where the unopened box of Triscuits is stashed, what half-read book is holding its place on the bedside table, exactly where the old wool shirt is hanging on a closet hook. At home, waves of clutter sweep into the house on a daily tide, stranding packages, mail, newspapers, cassettes, coupons, and folders on chairs, tables, and stair steps. Here at Wind Whistle, the beach remains relatively bare.

As I write these words, I am seated at my city desk, which is heaped with papers and unanswered mail. Thinking about Wind Whistle, I get lonely for it. I look out my window at pavement and wish I were gazing into the tangle of trees outside the window at Lake Pepin. If other city-dwellers share my kind of cabin fever, enough passion is raging in all of us to melt every snow of early spring.

Working with a gifted architect, who most happily was also my husband, I now live in a house that suits me perfectly. When James and I talked about titles for this book, he suggested *Falling in Love*, because he knew how a satisfied client feels about a house. No, I said, neither good design nor lasting love is that easy. But both are worth the effort.

For readers who may be about to embark on working with an architect to plan a house of their own, we wish them a joyous trip. We hope their particular castle in the air will turn out to have solid foundations—as well as a pleasing and functional form, a roof that doesn't leak, a bathroom with a window, and all the other details that are part of successful house design.

APPE**N**DIX A

LIST OF AMERICAN
INSTITUTE OF ARCHITECTS OFFICES

The American Institute of Architects (AIA) is a professional organization of architects. Its headquarters are at 1735 New York Avenue,
NW, Washington, DC 20006. The AIA has component chapters throughout the United States, whose telephone numbers are listed in the yellow pages under "Architects."

I often say that because of the necessarily competitive nature of our
profession, the AIA is the one group that brings architects together in
anything other than a "kill" situation, an overstatement that is rooted in
truth. I have great respect for the AIA and work hard within my state
organization for causes that affect all of us, such as design review
boards and continuing education.

The following list of affiliates will provide ready access to this group
of my fellow architects.

Alabama Council/AIA
PO Box 237
Montgomery, AL 36101
(205) 264-3037

Alaska Chapter/AIA
1113 West Firewood Ln.
Anchorage, AK 99503
(907) 276-2834

AIA Arizona
3738 North 16th St.
Phoenix, AZ 85016
(602) 279-0032

Arkansas Chapter/AIA
1123 South University
Little Rock, AR 72204
(501) 663-8820

California Council/AIA
1303 J St.
Sacramento, CA 95814
(916) 448-9082

AIA Colorado
1459 Pennsylvania Ave.
Denver, CO 80203
(303) 831-6183

Connecticut Society of Architects/AIA
87 Willow St.
New Haven, CT 06511-2627
(203) 865-2195

Delaware Society of Architects/AIA
1300 North Market St.
Wilmington, DE 19801
(302) 658-8045

Washington Chapter/AIA
1777 Church St., NW
Washington, DC 20036
(202) 667-1798

Florida Association/AIA
104 East Jefferson St.
Tallahassee, FL 32302
(904) 222-7590

Georgia Association/AIA
Colony Square Mall
1197 Peachtree St., NE
Atlanta, GA 30361
(404) 873-3207

Hawaii Council/AIA
1128 Nuuanu Ave.
Honolulu, HI 96817
(808) 545-4242

Idaho Chapter/AIA
405 South 8th St.
Boise, ID 83702
(208) 345-3072

Illinois Council/AIA
520 South 2nd St., 802 Lincoln Tower
Springfield, IL 62701
(217) 522-2309

Indiana Society of Architects/AIA
47 South Pennsylvania St.
Indianapolis, IN 46204
(317) 634-6993

Iowa Chapter/AIA
512 Walnut St.
Des Moines, IA 50309
(515) 244-7502

Kansas Society of Architects/AIA
700 Jackson St.
Topeka, KS 66603
(913) 357-5308

Kentucky Society of Architects/AIA
209 East High St.
Lexington, KY 40507
(606) 233-7671

Louisiana Architects Association/AIA
521 America St.
Baton Rouge, LA 70802
(504) 387-5579

Maine Chapter/AIA
3 Sylvan Way
Manchester, ME 04351
(207) 623-1218

Baltimore Chapter/AIA
11½ West Chase St.
Baltimore, MD 21201
(301) 625-2585

Massachusetts State Association of
Architects/AIA
52 Broad St.
Boston, MA 02109
(617) 951-1433

Michigan Society of Architects/AIA
553 East Jefferson St.
Detroit, MI 48226
(313) 965-4100

Minnesota Society of Architects/AIA
International Market Square
275 Market St.
Minneapolis, MN 55405
(612) 338-6763

Mississippi Chapter/AIA
812 North President St.
Jackson, MS 39202
(601) 948-6735

Missouri Council of Architects/AIA
204A East High St.
Jefferson City, MO 65101
(314) 635-8555

Montana Chapter/AIA
PO Box 20996
Billings, MT 59104
(406) 259-7300

Las Vegas Chapter/AIA
4505 South Maryland Pkwy.
Las Vegas, NV 89154
(702) 739-0936

Northern Nevada Chapter/AIA
115 West Plumb Ln.
Reno, NV 89509
(702) 329-7049

Nebraska Society of Architects/AIA
102 Architecture Hall
University of Nebraska—Lincoln
PO Box 80045
Lincoln, NE 68501-0045
(402) 472-1456

New Hampshire Chapter/AIA
76 South State St.
PO Box 1382
Concord, NH 03302-1382
(603) 228-0050

New Jersey Society of Architects/AIA
900 Route 9
Woodbridge, NJ 07095
(201) 636-5680

New Mexico Society/AIA
Albuquerque Chapter/AIA
110 2nd St., SW
Albuquerque, NM 87102
(505) 842-8744

New York State Association of
Architects/AIA
235 Lark St.
Albany, NY 12210
(518) 449-3334

North Carolina Chapter/AIA
115 West Morgan St.
Raleigh, NC 27601
(919) 833-6656

North Dakota Chapter/AIA
PO Box 1403
Fargo, ND 58107
(701) 235-4918

Architects Society of Ohio/AIA
17 South High St.
Columbus, OH 43215
(614) 221-0338

Central Oklahoma Chapter/AIA
405 NW 15th St.
Oklahoma City, OK 73103
(405) 525-7897

Eastern Oklahoma Chapter/AIA
2210-R South Main St.
Tulsa, OK 74114
(918) 583-0013

Oregon Council of Architects/AIA
1207 SW 6th Ave.
Portland, OR 97204
(503) 223-2330

Pennsylvania Society of Architects/AIA
PO Box 5570
Harrisburg, PA 17110-5570
(717) 236-4055

Puerto Rico Chapter/AIA
PO Box 3756
Hato Rey, PR 00919
(809) 758-4409

Rhode Island Chapter/AIA
The Arcade, Box 5
Providence, RI 02903
(401) 272-6418

South Carolina Chapter/AIA
1522 Richland St.
Columbia, SC 29201
(803) 252-6050

South Dakota Society/AIA
PO Box 1596
Sioux Falls, SD 57101
(605) 334-2422

Tennessee Society of Architects/AIA
530 Church St.
Nashville, TN 37219
(615) 256-2311

Texas Society of Architects/AIA
114 West 7th St.
Austin, TX 78701
(512) 478-7386

Salt Lake Chapter/AIA
1819 E. 1300 South
Salt Lake City, UT 84108
(801) 582-8207

Vermont Chapter/AIA
RFD #1, Box 67
Waitsfield, VT 05673
(802) 496-3761

Virginia Society/AIA
James River Chapter/AIA
15 South 5th St.
Richmond, VA 23219
(804) 644-3041

Washington Council/AIA
McCleary Mansion
111 West 21st Ave., SW
Olympia, WA 98501
(206) 943-6012

West Virginia Society of Architects/AIA
PO Box 813
Charleston, WV 25323
(304) 344-9872

Wisconsin Society of Architects/AIA
321 South Hamilton St.
Madison, WI 53703
(608) 257-8477

APPENDIX B

SAMPLE CONTRACT

Note: This is a sample contract of the kind I use with my clients.

THE AMERICAN INSTITUTE OF ARCHITECTS

AIA Document B141

Standard Form of Agreement Between Owner and Architect

1977 EDITION

THIS DOCUMENT HAS IMPORTANT LEGAL CONSEQUENCES; CONSULTATION WITH AN ATTORNEY IS ENCOURAGED WITH RESPECT TO ITS COMPLETION OR MODIFICATION

AGREEMENT

made as of the   Ninth   day of   October   in the year of Nineteen Hundred and   Ninety Ninety

BETWEEN the Owner:

and the Architect:

    The Stageberg Partners, Inc.

For the following Project:
(Include detailed description of Project location and scope.)

    A residence

The Owner and the Architect agree as set forth below.

AIA DOCUMENT B141 • OWNER-ARCHITECT AGREEMENT • THIRTEENTH EDITION • JULY 1977 • AIA® • © 1977
THE AMERICAN INSTITUTE OF ARCHITECTS, 1735 NEW YORK AVENUE, N.W., WASHINGTON, D.C. 20006

B141-1977

TERMS AND CONDITIONS OF AGREEMENT BETWEEN OWNER AND ARCHITECT

ARTICLE 1

ARCHITECT'S SERVICES AND RESPONSIBILITIES

BASIC SERVICES

The Architect's Basic Services consist of the five phases described in Paragraphs 1.1 through 1.5 and include normal structural, mechanical and electrical engineering services and any other services included in Article 15 as part of Basic Services.

1.1 SCHEMATIC DESIGN PHASE

1.1.1 The Architect shall review the program furnished by the Owner to ascertain the requirements of the Project and shall review the understanding of such requirements with the Owner.

1.1.2 The Architect shall provide a preliminary evaluation of the program and the Project budget requirements, each in terms of the other, subject to the limitations set forth in Subparagraph 3.2.1.

1.1.3 The Architect shall review with the Owner alternative approaches to design and construction of the Project.

1.1.4 Based on the mutually agreed upon program and Project budget requirements, the Architect shall prepare, for approval by the Owner, Schematic Design Documents consisting of drawings and other documents illustrating the scale and relationship of Project components.

1.1.5 The Architect shall submit to the Owner a Statement of Probable Construction Cost based on current area, volume or other unit costs.

1.2 DESIGN DEVELOPMENT PHASE

1.2.1 Based on the approved Schematic Design Documents and any adjustments authorized by the Owner in the program or Project budget, the Architect shall prepare, for approval by the Owner, Design Development Documents consisting of drawings and other documents to fix and describe the size and character of the entire Project as to architectural, structural, mechanical and electrical systems, materials and such other elements as may be appropriate.

1.2.2 The Architect shall submit to the Owner a further Statement of Probable Construction Cost.

1.3 CONSTRUCTION DOCUMENTS PHASE

1.3.1 Based on the approved Design Development Documents and any further adjustments in the scope or quality of the Project or in the Project budget authorized by the Owner, the Architect shall prepare, for approval by the Owner, Construction Documents consisting of Drawings and Specifications setting forth in detail the requirements for the construction of the Project.

1.3.2 The Architect shall assist the Owner in the preparation of the necessary bidding information, bidding forms, the Conditions of the Contract, and the form of Agreement between the Owner and the Contractor.

1.3.3 The Architect shall advise the Owner of any adjust-

ments to previous Statements of Probable Construction Cost indicated by changes in requirements or general market conditions.

1.3.4 The Architect shall assist the Owner in connection with the Owner's responsibility for filing documents required for the approval of governmental authorities having jurisdiction over the Project.

1.4 BIDDING OR NEGOTIATION PHASE

1.4.1 The Architect, following the Owner's approval of the Construction Documents and of the latest Statement of Probable Construction Cost, shall assist the Owner in obtaining bids or negotiated proposals, and assist in awarding and preparing contracts for construction.

1.5 CONSTRUCTION PHASE—ADMINISTRATION OF THE CONSTRUCTION CONTRACT

1.5.1 The Construction Phase will commence with the award of the Contract for Construction and, together with the Architect's obligation to provide Basic Services under this Agreement, will terminate when final payment to the Contractor is due, or in the absence of a final Certificate for Payment or of such due date, sixty days after the Date of Substantial Completion of the Work, whichever occurs first.

1.5.2 Unless otherwise provided in this Agreement and incorporated in the Contract Documents, the Architect shall provide administration of the Contract for Construction as set forth below and in the edition of AIA Document A201, General Conditions of the Contract for Construction, current as of the date of this Agreement.

1.5.3 The Architect shall be a representative of the Owner during the Construction Phase, and shall advise and consult with the Owner. Instructions to the Contractor shall be forwarded through the Architect. The Architect shall have authority to act on behalf of the Owner only to the extent provided in the Contract Documents unless otherwise modified by written instrument in accordance with Subparagraph 1.5.16.

1.5.4 The Architect shall visit the site at intervals appropriate to the stage of construction or as otherwise agreed by the Architect in writing to become generally familiar with the progress and quality of the Work and to determine in general if the Work is proceeding in accordance with the Contract Documents. However, the Architect shall not be required to make exhaustive or continuous on-site inspections to check the quality or quantity of the Work. On the basis of such on-site observations as an architect, the Architect shall keep the Owner informed of the progress and quality of the Work, and shall endeavor to guard the Owner against defects and deficiencies in the Work of the Contractor.

1.5.5 The Architect shall not have control or charge of and shall not be responsible for construction means, methods, techniques, sequences or procedures, or for safety precautions and programs in connection with the Work, for the acts or omissions of the Contractor, Sub-

AIA DOCUMENT B141 • OWNER-ARCHITECT AGREEMENT • THIRTEENTH EDITION • JULY 1977 • AIA® • © 1977
THE AMERICAN INSTITUTE OF ARCHITECTS, 1735 NEW YORK AVENUE, N.W., WASHINGTON, D.C. 20006

B141-1977

APPENDIX B

contractors or any other persons performing any of the Work, or for the failure of any of them to carry out the Work in accordance with the Contract Documents.

1.5.6 The Architect shall at all times have access to the Work wherever it is in preparation or progress.

1.5.7 The Architect shall determine the amounts owing to the Contractor based on observations at the site and on evaluations of the Contractor's Applications for Payment, and shall issue Certificates for Payment in such amounts, as provided in the Contract Documents.

1.5.8 The issuance of a Certificate for Payment shall constitute a representation by the Architect to the Owner, based on the Architect's observations at the site as provided in Subparagraph 1.5.4 and on the data comprising the Contractor's Application for Payment, that the Work has progressed to the point indicated; that, to the best of the Architect's knowledge, information and belief, the quality of the Work is in accordance with the Contract Documents (subject to an evaluation of the Work for conformance with the Contract Documents upon Substantial Completion, to the results of any subsequent tests required by or performed under the Contract Documents, to minor deviations from the Contract Documents correctable prior to completion, and to any specific qualifications stated in the Certificate for Payment); and that the Contractor is entitled to payment in the amount certified. However, the issuance of a Certificate for Payment shall not be a representation that the Architect has made any examination to ascertain how and for what purpose the Contractor has used the moneys paid on account of the Contract Sum.

1.5.9 The Architect shall be the interpreter of the requirements of the Contract Documents and the judge of the performance thereunder by both the Owner and Contractor. The Architect shall render interpretations necessary for the proper execution or progress of the Work with reasonable promptness on written request of either the Owner or the Contractor, and shall render written decisions, within a reasonable time, on all claims, disputes and other matters in question between the Owner and the Contractor relating to the execution or progress of the Work or the interpretation of the Contract Documents.

1.5.10 Interpretations and decisions of the Architect shall be consistent with the intent of and reasonably inferable from the Contract Documents and shall be in written or graphic form. In the capacity of interpreter and judge, the Architect shall endeavor to secure faithful performance by both the Owner and the Contractor, shall not show partiality to either, and shall not be liable for the result of any interpretation or decision rendered in good faith in such capacity.

1.5.11 The Architect's decisions in matters relating to artistic effect shall be final if consistent with the intent of the Contract Documents. The Architect's decisions on any other claims, disputes or other matters, including those in question between the Owner and the Contractor, shall be subject to arbitration as provided in this Agreement and in the Contract Documents.

1.5.12 The Architect shall have authority to reject Work which does not conform to the Contract Documents. Whenever, in the Architect's reasonable opinion, it is

necessary or advisable for the implementation of the intent of the Contract Documents, the Architect will have authority to require special inspection or testing of the Work in accordance with the provisions of the Contract Documents, whether or not such Work be then fabricated, installed or completed.

1.5.13 The Architect shall review and approve or take other appropriate action upon the Contractor's submittals such as Shop Drawings, Product Data and Samples, but only for conformance with the design concept of the Work and with the information given in the Contract Documents. Such action shall be taken with reasonable promptness so as to cause no delay. The Architect's approval of a specific item shall not indicate approval of an assembly of which the item is a component.

1.5.14 The Architect shall prepare Change Orders for the Owner's approval and execution in accordance with the Contract Documents, and shall have authority to order minor changes in the Work not involving an adjustment in the Contract Sum or an extension of the Contract Time which are not inconsistent with the intent of the Contract Documents.

1.5.15 The Architect shall conduct inspections to determine the Dates of Substantial Completion and final completion, shall receive and forward to the Owner for the Owner's review written warranties and related documents required by the Contract Documents and assembled by the Contractor, and shall issue a final Certificate for Payment.

1.5.16 The extent of the duties, responsibilities and limitations of authority of the Architect as the Owner's representative during construction shall not be modified or extended without written consent of the Owner, the Contractor and the Architect.

1.6 PROJECT REPRESENTATION BEYOND BASIC SERVICES

1.6.1 If the Owner and Architect agree that more extensive representation at the site than is described in Paragraph 1.5 shall be provided, the Architect shall provide one or more Project Representatives to assist the Architect in carrying out such responsibilities at the site.

1.6.2 Such Project Representatives shall be selected, employed and directed by the Architect, and the Architect shall be compensated therefor as mutually agreed between the Owner and the Architect as set forth in an exhibit appended to this Agreement, which shall describe the duties, responsibilities and limitations of authority of such Project Representatives.

1.6.3 Through the observations by such Project Representatives, the Architect shall endeavor to provide further protection for the Owner against defects and deficiencies in the Work, but the furnishing of such project representation shall not modify the rights, responsibilities or obligations of the Architect as described in Paragraph 1.5.

1.7 ADDITIONAL SERVICES

The following Services are not included in Basic Services unless so identified in Article 15. They shall be provided if authorized or confirmed in writing by the Owner, and they shall be paid for by the Owner as provided in this Agreement, in addition to the compensation for Basic Services.

1.7.1 Providing analyses of the Owner's needs, and programming the requirements of the Project.

1.7.2 Providing financial feasibility or other special studies.

1.7.3 Providing planning surveys, site evaluations, environmental studies or comparative studies of prospective sites, and preparing special surveys, studies and submissions required for approvals of governmental authorities or others having jurisdiction over the Project.

1.7.4 Providing services relative to future facilities, systems and equipment which are not intended to be constructed during the Construction Phase.

1.7.5 Providing services to investigate existing conditions or facilities or to make measured drawings thereof, or to verify the accuracy of drawings or other information furnished by the Owner.

1.7.6 Preparing documents of alternate, separate or sequential bids or providing extra services in connection with bidding, negotiation or construction prior to the completion of the Construction Documents Phase, when requested by the Owner.

1.7.7 Providing coordination of Work performed by separate contractors or by the Owner's own forces.

1.7.8 Providing services in connection with the work of a construction manager or separate consultants retained by the Owner.

1.7.9 Providing Detailed Estimates of Construction Cost, analyses of owning and operating costs, or detailed quantity surveys or inventories of material, equipment and labor.

1.7.10 Providing interior design and other similar services required for or in connection with the selection, procurement or installation of furniture, furnishings and related equipment.

1.7.11 Providing services for planning tenant or rental spaces.

1.7.12 Making revisions in Drawings, Specifications or other documents when such revisions are inconsistent with written approvals or instructions previously given, are required by the enactment or revision of codes, laws or regulations subsequent to the preparation of such documents or are due to other causes not solely within the control of the Architect.

1.7.13 Preparing Drawings, Specifications and supporting data and providing other services in connection with Change Orders to the extent that the adjustment in the Basic Compensation resulting from the adjusted Construction Cost is not commensurate with the services required of the Architect, provided such Change Orders are required by causes not solely within the control of the Architect.

1.7.14 Making investigations, surveys, valuations, inventories or detailed appraisals of existing facilities, and services required in connection with construction performed by the Owner.

1.7.15 Providing consultation concerning replacement of any Work damaged by fire or other cause during con-

struction, and furnishing services as may be required in connection with the replacement of such Work.

1.7.16 Providing services made necessary by the default of the Contractor, or by major defects or deficiencies in the Work of the Contractor, or by failure of performance of either the Owner or Contractor under the Contract for Construction.

1.7.17 Preparing a set of reproducible record drawings showing significant changes in the Work made during construction based on marked-up prints, drawings and other data furnished by the Contractor to the Architect.

1.7.18 Providing extensive assistance in the utilization of any equipment or system such as initial start-up or testing, adjusting and balancing, preparation of operation and maintenance manuals, training personnel for operation and maintenance, and consultation during operation.

1.7.19 Providing services after issuance to the Owner of the final Certificate for Payment, or in the absence of a final Certificate for Payment, more than sixty days after the Date of Substantial Completion of the Work.

1.7.20 Preparing to serve or serving as an expert witness in connection with any public hearing, arbitration proceeding or legal proceeding.

1.7.21 Providing services of consultants for other than the normal architectural, structural, mechanical and electrical engineering services for the Project.

1.7.22 Providing any other services not otherwise included in this Agreement or not customarily furnished in accordance with generally accepted architectural practice.

1.8 TIME

1.8.1 The Architect shall perform Basic and Additional Services as expeditiously as is consistent with professional skill and care and the orderly progress of the Work. Upon request of the Owner, the Architect shall submit for the Owner's approval a schedule for the performance of the Architect's services which shall be adjusted as required as the Project proceeds, and shall include allowances for periods of time required for the Owner's review and approval of submissions and for approvals of authorities having jurisdiction over the Project. This schedule, when approved by the Owner, shall not, except for reasonable cause, be exceeded by the Architect.

ARTICLE 2

THE OWNER'S RESPONSIBILITIES

2.1 The Owner shall provide full information regarding requirements for the Project including a program, which shall set forth the Owner's design objectives, constraints and criteria, including space requirements and relationships, flexibility and expandability, special equipment and systems and site requirements.

2.2 If the Owner provides a budget for the Project it shall include contingencies for bidding, changes in the Work during construction, and other costs which are the responsibility of the Owner, including those described in this Article 2 and in Subparagraph 3.1.2. The Owner shall, at the request of the Architect, provide a statement of funds available for the Project, and their source.

AIA DOCUMENT B141 • OWNER-ARCHITECT AGREEMENT • THIRTEENTH EDITION • JULY 1977 • AIA® • © 1977
THE AMERICAN INSTITUTE OF ARCHITECTS, 1735 NEW YORK AVENUE, N.W., WASHINGTON, D.C. 20006   **B141-1977**

2.3 The Owner shall designate, when necessary, a representative authorized to act in the Owner's behalf with respect to the Project. The Owner or such authorized representative shall examine the documents submitted by the Architect and shall render decisions pertaining thereto promptly, to avoid unreasonable delay in the progress of the Architect's services.

2.4 The Owner shall furnish a legal description and a certified land survey of the site, giving, as applicable, grades and lines of streets, alleys, pavements and adjoining property; rights-of-way, restrictions, easements, encroachments, zoning, deed restrictions, boundaries and contours of the site; locations, dimensions and complete data pertaining to existing buildings, other improvements and trees; and full information concerning available service and utility lines both public and private, above and below grade, including inverts and depths.

2.5 The Owner shall furnish the services of soil engineers or other consultants when such services are deemed necessary by the Architect. Such services shall include test borings, test pits, soil bearing values, percolation tests, air and water pollution tests, ground corrosion and resistivity tests, including necessary operations for determining subsoil, air and water conditions, with reports and appropriate professional recommendations.

2.6 The Owner shall furnish structural, mechanical, chemical and other laboratory tests, inspections and reports as required by law or the Contract Documents.

2.7 The Owner shall furnish all legal, accounting and insurance counseling services as may be necessary at any time for the Project, including such auditing services as the Owner may require to verify the Contractor's Applications for Payment or to ascertain how or for what purposes the Contractor uses the moneys paid by or on behalf of the Owner.

2.8 The services, information, surveys and reports required by Paragraphs 2.4 through 2.7 inclusive shall be furnished at the Owner's expense, and the Architect shall be entitled to rely upon the accuracy and completeness thereof.

2.9 If the Owner observes or otherwise becomes aware of any fault or defect in the Project or nonconformance with the Contract Documents, prompt written notice thereof shall be given by the Owner to the Architect.

2.10 The Owner shall furnish required information and services and shall render approvals and decisions as expeditiously as necessary for the orderly progress of the Architect's services and of the Work.

ARTICLE 3

CONSTRUCTION COST

3.1 DEFINITION

3.1.1 The Construction Cost shall be the total cost or estimated cost to the Owner of all elements of the Project designed or specified by the Architect.

3.1.2 The Construction Cost shall include at current market rates, including a reasonable allowance for overhead and profit, the cost of labor and materials furnished by the Owner and any equipment which has been de-

signed, specified, selected or specially provided for by the Architect.

3.1.3 Construction Cost does not include the compensation of the Architect and the Architect's consultants, the cost of the land, rights-of-way, or other costs which are the responsibility of the Owner as provided in Article 2.

3.2 RESPONSIBILITY FOR CONSTRUCTION COST

3.2.1 Evaluations of the Owner's Project budget, Statements of Probable Construction Cost and Detailed Estimates of Construction Cost, if any, prepared by the Architect, represent the Architect's best judgment as a design professional familiar with the construction industry. It is recognized, however, that neither the Architect nor the Owner has control over the cost of labor, materials or equipment, over the Contractor's methods of determining bid prices, or over competitive bidding, market or negotiating conditions. Accordingly, the Architect cannot and does not warrant or represent that bids or negotiated prices will not vary from the Project budget proposed, established or approved by the Owner, if any, or from any Statement of Probable Construction Cost or other cost estimate or evaluation prepared by the Architect.

3.2.2 No fixed limit of Construction Cost shall be established as a condition of this Agreement by the furnishing, proposal or establishment of a Project budget under Subparagraph 1.1.2 or Paragraph 2.2 or otherwise, unless such fixed limit has been agreed upon in writing and signed by the parties hereto. If such a fixed limit has been established, the Architect shall be permitted to include contingencies for design, bidding and price escalation, to determine what materials, equipment, component systems and types of construction are to be included in the Contract Documents, to make reasonable adjustments in the scope of the Project and to include in the Contract Documents alternate bids to adjust the Construction Cost to the fixed limit. Any such fixed limit shall be increased in the amount of any increase in the Contract Sum occurring after execution of the Contract for Construction.

3.2.3 If the Bidding or Negotiation Phase has not commenced within three months after the Architect submits the Construction Documents to the Owner, any Project budget or fixed limit of Construction Cost shall be adjusted to reflect any change in the general level of prices in the construction industry between the date of submission of the Construction Documents to the Owner and the date on which proposals are sought.

3.2.4 If a Project budget or fixed limit of Construction Cost (adjusted as provided in Subparagraph 3.2.3) is exceeded by the lowest bona fide bid or negotiated proposal, the Owner shall (1) give written approval of an increase in such fixed limit, (2) authorize rebidding or renegotiating of the Project within a reasonable time, (3) if the Project is abandoned, terminate in accordance with Paragraph 10.2, or (4) cooperate in revising the Project scope and quality as required to reduce the Construction Cost. In the case of (4), provided a fixed limit of Construction Cost has been established as a condition of this Agreement, the Architect, without additional charge, shall modify the Drawings and Specifications as necessary to comply with the fixed limit. The providing of such service shall be the limit of the Architect's responsibility arising from the establishment of such fixed limit, and having done so, the Architect shall be entitled to compensation for all services performed, in accordance with this Agreement, whether or not the Construction Phase is commenced.

ARTICLE 4

DIRECT PERSONNEL EXPENSE

4.1 Direct Personnel Expense is defined as the direct salaries of all the Architect's personnel engaged on the Project, and the portion of the cost of their mandatory and customary contributions and benefits related thereto, such as employment taxes and other statutory employee benefits, insurance, sick leave, holidays, vacations, pensions and similar contributions and benefits.

ARTICLE 5

REIMBURSABLE EXPENSES

5.1 Reimbursable Expenses are in addition to the Compensation for Basic and Additional Services and include actual expenditures made by the Architect and the Architect's employees and consultants in the interest of the Project for the expenses listed in the following Subparagraphs:

5.1.1 Expense of transportation in connection with the Project; living expenses in connection with out-of-town travel; long distance communications; and fees paid for securing approval of authorities having jurisdiction over the Project.

5.1.2 Expense of reproductions, postage and handling of Drawings, Specifications and other documents, excluding reproductions for the office use of the Architect and the Architect's consultants.

5.1.3 Expense of data processing and photographic production techniques when used in connection with Additional Services.

5.1.4 If authorized in advance by the Owner, expense of overtime work requiring higher than regular rates.

5.1.5 Expense of renderings, models and mock-ups requested by the Owner.

5.1.6 Expense of any additional insurance coverage or limits, including professional liability insurance, requested by the Owner in excess of that normally carried by the Architect and the Architect's consultants.

ARTICLE 6

PAYMENTS TO THE ARCHITECT

6.1 **PAYMENTS ON ACCOUNT OF BASIC SERVICES**

6.1.1 An initial payment as set forth in Paragraph 14.1 is the minimum payment under this Agreement.

6.1.2 Subsequent payments for Basic Services shall be made monthly and shall be in proportion to services performed within each Phase of services, on the basis set forth in Article 14.

6.1.3 If and to the extent that the Contract Time initially established in the Contract for Construction is exceeded or extended through no fault of the Architect, compensation for any Basic Services required for such extended period of Administration of the Construction Contract shall be computed as set forth in Paragraph 14.4 for Additional Services.

6.1.4 When compensation is based on a percentage of Construction Cost, and any portions of the Project are deleted or otherwise not constructed, compensation for such portions of the Project shall be payable to the extent services are performed on such portions, in accordance with the schedule set forth in Subparagraph 14.2.2, based on (1) the lowest bona fide bid or negotiated proposal or, (2) if no such bid or proposal is received, the most recent Statement of Probable Construction Cost or Detailed Estimate of Construction Cost for such portions of the Project.

6.2 **PAYMENTS ON ACCOUNT OF ADDITIONAL SERVICES**

6.2.1 Payments on account of the Architect's Additional Services as defined in Paragraph 1.7 and for Reimbursable Expenses as defined in Article 5 shall be made monthly upon presentation of the Architect's statement of services rendered or expenses incurred.

6.3 **PAYMENTS WITHHELD**

6.3.1 No deductions shall be made from the Architect's compensation on account of penalty, liquidated damages or other sums withheld from payments to contractors, or on account of the cost of changes in the Work other than those for which the Architect is held legally liable.

6.4 **PROJECT SUSPENSION OR TERMINATION**

6.4.1 If the Project is suspended or abandoned in whole or in part for more than three months, the Architect shall be compensated for all services performed prior to receipt of written notice from the Owner of such suspension or abandonment, together with Reimbursable Expenses then due and all Termination Expenses as defined in Paragraph 10.4. If the Project is resumed after being suspended for more than three months, the Architect's compensation shall be equitably adjusted.

ARTICLE 7

ARCHITECT'S ACCOUNTING RECORDS

7.1 Records of Reimbursable Expenses and expenses pertaining to Additional Services and services performed on the basis of a Multiple of Direct Personnel Expense shall be kept on the basis of generally accepted accounting principles and shall be available to the Owner or the Owner's authorized representative at mutually convenient times.

ARTICLE 8

OWNERSHIP AND USE OF DOCUMENTS

8.1 Drawings and Specifications as instruments of service are and shall remain the property of the Architect whether the Project for which they are made is executed or not. The Owner shall be permitted to retain copies, including reproducible copies, of Drawings and Specifications for information and reference in connection with the Owner's use and occupancy of the Project. The Drawings and Specifications shall not be used by the Owner on other projects, for additions to this Project, or for completion of this Project by others provided the Architect is not in default under this Agreement, except by agreement in writing and with appropriate compensation to the Architect.

8.2 Submission or distribution to meet official regulatory requirements or for other purposes in connection with the Project is not to be construed as publication in derogation of the Architect's rights.

ARTICLE 9

ARBITRATION

9.1 All claims, disputes and other matters in question between the parties to this Agreement, arising out of or relating to this Agreement or the breach thereof, shall be decided by arbitration in accordance with the Construction Industry Arbitration Rules of the American Arbitration Association then obtaining unless the parties mutually agree otherwise. No arbitration, arising out of or relating to this Agreement, shall include, by consolidation, joinder or in any other manner, any additional person not a party to this Agreement except by written consent containing a specific reference to this Agreement and signed by the Architect, the Owner, and any other person sought to be joined. Any consent to arbitration involving an additional person or persons shall not constitute consent to arbitration of any dispute not described therein or with any person not named or described therein. This Agreement to arbitrate and any agreement to arbitrate with an additional person or persons duly consented to by the parties to this Agreement shall be specifically enforceable under the prevailing arbitration law.

9.2 Notice of the demand for arbitration shall be filed in writing with the other party to this Agreement and with the American Arbitration Association. The demand shall be made within a reasonable time after the claim, dispute or other matter in question has arisen. In no event shall the demand for arbitration be made after the date when institution of legal or equitable proceedings based on such claim, dispute or other matter in question would be barred by the applicable statute of limitations.

9.3 The award rendered by the arbitrators shall be final, and judgment may be entered upon it in accordance with applicable law in any court having jurisdiction thereof.

ARTICLE 10

TERMINATION OF AGREEMENT

10.1 This Agreement may be terminated by either party upon seven days' written notice should the other party fail substantially to perform in accordance with its terms through no fault of the party initiating the termination.

10.2 This Agreement may be terminated by the Owner upon at least seven days' written notice to the Architect in the event that the Project is permanently abandoned.

10.3 In the event of termination not the fault of the Architect, the Architect shall be compensated for all services performed to termination date, together with Reimbursable Expenses then due and all Termination Expenses as defined in Paragraph 10.4.

10.4 Termination Expenses include expenses directly attributable to termination for which the Architect is not otherwise compensated, plus an amount computed as a percentage of the total Basic and Additional Compensation earned to the time of termination, as follows:

.1 20 percent if termination occurs during the Schematic Design Phase; or

.2 10 percent if termination occurs during the Design Development Phase; or

.3 5 percent if termination occurs during any subsequent phase.

ARTICLE 11

MISCELLANEOUS PROVISIONS

11.1 Unless otherwise specified, this Agreement shall be governed by the law of the principal place of business of the Architect.

11.2 Terms in this Agreement shall have the same meaning as those in AIA Document A201, General Conditions of the Contract for Construction, current as of the date of this Agreement.

11.3 As between the parties to this Agreement: as to all acts or failures to act by either party to this Agreement, any applicable statute of limitations shall commence to run and any alleged cause of action shall be deemed to have accrued in any and all events not later than the relevant Date of Substantial Completion of the Work, and as to any acts or failures to act occurring after the relevant Date of Substantial Completion, not later than the date of issuance of the final Certificate for Payment.

11.4 The Owner and the Architect waive all rights against each other and against the contractors, consultants, agents and employees of the other for damages covered by any property insurance during construction as set forth in the edition of AIA Document A201, General Conditions, current as of the date of this Agreement. The Owner and the Architect each shall require appropriate similar waivers from their contractors, consultants and agents.

ARTICLE 12

SUCCESSORS AND ASSIGNS

12.1 The Owner and the Architect, respectively, bind themselves, their partners, successors, assigns and legal representatives to the other party to this Agreement and to the partners, successors, assigns and legal representatives of such other party with respect to all covenants of this Agreement. Neither the Owner nor the Architect shall assign, sublet or transfer any interest in this Agreement without the written consent of the other.

ARTICLE 13

EXTENT OF AGREEMENT

13.1 This Agreement represents the entire and integrated agreement between the Owner and the Architect and supersedes all prior negotiations, representations or agreements, either written or oral. This Agreement may be amended only by written instrument signed by both Owner and Architect.

ARTICLE 14

BASIS OF COMPENSATION

The Owner shall compensate the Architect for the Scope of Services provided, in accordance with Article 6, Payments to the Architect, and the other Terms and Conditions of this Agreement, as follows:

14.1 AN INITIAL PAYMENT of   none   dollars ($)

shall be made upon execution of this Agreement and credited to the Owner's account as follows:

14.2 BASIC COMPENSATION

14.2.1 FOR BASIC SERVICES, as described in Paragraphs 1.1 through 1.5, and any other services included in Article 15 as part of Basic Services, Basic Compensation shall be computed as follows:

(Here insert basis of compensation, including fixed amounts, multiples or percentages, and identify Phases to which particular methods of compensation apply, if necessary.)

10% of construction costs

14.2.2 Where compensation is based on a Stipulated Sum or Percentage of Construction Cost, payments for Basic Services shall be made as provided in Subparagraph 6.1.2, so that Basic Compensation for each Phase shall equal the following percentages of the total Basic Compensation payable:

(Include any additional Phases as appropriate.)

Schematic Design Phase:	percent (20 %)
Design Development Phase:	percent (15 %)
Construction Documents Phase:	percent (40 %)
Bidding or Negotiation Phase:	percent (05 %)
Construction Phase:	percent (20 %)

14.3 FOR PROJECT REPRESENTATION BEYOND BASIC SERVICES, as described in Paragraph 1.6, Compensation shall be computed separately in accordance with Subparagraph 1.6.2.

14.4 COMPENSATION FOR ADDITIONAL SERVICES

14.4.1 FOR ADDITIONAL SERVICES OF THE ARCHITECT, as described in Paragraph 1.7, and any other services included in Article 15 as part of Additional Services, but excluding Additional Services of consultants, Compensation shall be computed as follows:

(Here insert basis of compensation, including rates and/or multiples of Direct Personnel Expense for Principals and employees, and identify Principals and classify employees, if required. Identify specific services to which particular methods of compensation apply, if necessary.)

Senior Architect	$85.00
Architect	$60.00
Assistant	varies

14.4.2 FOR ADDITIONAL SERVICES OF CONSULTANTS, including additional structural, mechanical and electrical engineering services and those provided under Subparagraph 1.7.21 or identified in Article 15 as part of Additional Services, a multiple of (none) times the amounts billed to the Architect for such services.

(Identify specific types of consultants in Article 15, if required.)

14.5 FOR REIMBURSABLE EXPENSES, as described in Article 5, and any other items included in Article 15 as Reimbursable Expenses, a multiple of (1.0) times the amounts expended by the Architect, the Architect's employees and consultants in the interest of the Project.

14.6 Payments due the Architect and unpaid under this Agreement shall bear interest from the date payment is due at the rate entered below, or in the absence thereof, at the legal rate prevailing at the principal place of business of the Architect. 12%

(Here insert any rate of interest agreed upon.)

(Usury laws and requirements under the Federal Truth in Lending Act, similar state and local consumer credit laws and other regulations at the Owner's and Architect's principal places of business, the location of the Project and elsewhere may affect the validity of this provision. Specific legal advice should be obtained with respect to deletion, modification, or other requirements such as written disclosures or waivers.)

14.7 The Owner and the Architect agree in accordance with the Terms and Conditions of this Agreement that:

14.7.1 IF THE SCOPE of the Project or of the Architect's Services is changed materially, the amounts of compensation shall be equitably adjusted.

14.7.2 IF THE SERVICES covered by this Agreement have not been completed within

(18 months of the date hereof, through no fault of the Architect, the amounts of compensation, rates and multiples set forth herein shall be equitably adjusted.

This Agreement entered into as of the day and year first written above.

OWNER   ARCHITECT

_____   _____
                                         The Stageberg Partners, Inc.
_____   _____

BY_____   BY James Stageberg

B141-1977   AIA DOCUMENT B141 • OWNER-ARCHITECT AGREEMENT • THIRTEENTH EDITION • JULY 1977 • AIA® • © 1977
THE AMERICAN INSTITUTE OF ARCHITECTS, 1735 NEW YORK AVENUE, N.W., WASHINGTON, D.C. 20006

Notice:

1. AIA copyrighted material has been reproduced with the permission of the American Institute of Architects under license number 91020. Permission expires February 28, 1992. FURTHER REPRODUCTION IS PROHIBITED.

2. Because AIA Documents are revised from time to time, users should ascertain from the AIA the current edition of this document.

3. Copies of the current edition of this AIA document may be purchased from The American Institute of Architects or its local distributors.

4. This document is intended for use as a "consumable" (consumables are further defined by Senate Report 94-473 on the Copyright Act of 1976). This document is not intended to be used as "model language" (language taken from an existing document and incorporated, without attribution, into a newly created document). Rather, it is a standard form which is intended to be modified by appending separate amendment sheets and/or fill in provided blank spaces.

A P **P** E N D I X C

S A M P L E S P E C I F I C A T I O N S

ARCHITECTS PLANNERS

the Stageberg Partners inc

115 N FOURTH ST   MINNEAPOLIS   MINNESOTA   55401   612/375-1399

MEMORANDUM

TO: Larry Smith/Mark Vogen

FROM: James Stageberg

REFERENCE: Toth/Stageberg - Wind Whistle

It is my hope to start our cabin by May 1. This will depend upon a
complete and accurate estimate of all costs involved. I will be getting
some of these and you will be getting most of them. The following list
are those I ask you to get at this time.

If you're certain about the work and cost competitiveness of some of the
subcontractors, one bid will be sufficient. Otherwise, get several bids
on the major items. I'll leave this to your discretion.

I'm not asking you to assume any financial responsibility for this
project. I do want an estimate of labor costs from you. I expect to pay
you for helping me secure these bids.

The viability of starting the cabin right away depends on the bottom
line. Please do your best to secure these prices in the form of bids and
estimates, as soon as possible.

Instructions to builder

Toth/Stageberg Cabin Retreat - Wind Whistle
Pepin County, Wisconsin

A. Excavation
    1. All excavation will include trenching for the footings and
        foundation, the extension of the waterline from the nearest
        point, and the laying of underground electrical cables. Note
        that there is no basement but only a crawl space. No dirt to be
        hauled away.

B. Lumber and materials
    1. All framing lumber to be Hem Fir #2 or better.
    2. All foundation walls to be treated 2/8 studs with treated 1/2"
        plywood exterior sheathing.
    3. All exterior wall studs above grade to be 2x6, all interior wall
        studs to be 2x4.
    4. All wall and roof sheathing to be 1/2" CDX plywood.
    5. All floor and roof joists to be as noted on framing plans.
    6. Provide bridging as required.
    7. Subflooring over joists to be 5/8" plywood CD grade.
    8. Provide 1/2" wafer board underlayment for carpet areas.
    9. Roof and wall shingles to be 3/8" butt #1 Cedar, 5" exposure on
        roof and wall areas.
    10. All the exterior walls, except for those two small areas to be
        shingled, will be 6" smooth redwood lap siding. All trim boards
        will be 1x4 R.W.
    11. All soffits to be 1x4, R.W. T & G V joint.
    12. All interior trim and door frames to be pine.
    13. The interior doors shall be good quality paint grade wood panel
        doors. The closet doors should be louvered pine.
    14. All manufactured windows to be wood.
    15. Provide 1x6 T & G V joint horizontal white oak siding throughout
        the interior walls as noted to the head of all doors and windows.
    16. Provide 2x12 beams, as shown, and continuous facia above windows
        for the L.R., D.R., B.R., and study of construction grade Fir,
        resawn. Provide 5/8" bolts and washers as shown.
    17. Provide 1x4, #2 pine, tongue and grove, flush joint boards from
        the top of the continuous 2x12 beam to the sloped roof and on all
        ceiling surfaces throughout the house, except #2 bedroom.
    18. The exterior deck joists and beams to be treated lumber.
    19. The exterior balcony railings to be steel.
    20. The exterior decks to be 1x4 R.W., spaced approximately 3/8"
        apart.
    21. The ladders to be constructed from clear redwood.
    22. Provide white oak base throughout all levels.
    23. Provide one exterior Lee Haven #16 entry door.
    24. Provide 1/2" sheetrock as noted on plans.

Builder Instructions

C. Plumbing

Provide all systems required for complete operation, ready to use. This includes water hook-up, drainage system, and fixtures, including 50 gallon hot water heater. Provide an allowance for a white sink, tub, toilet, and bidet.

Note in bid, manufacturer and number of all fixtures, and their cost.

D. Electrical

Provide all systems, wiring, and hook-up of all fixtures required for complete operation, ready to use according to the plan by the architect. Provide underground electrical service. Provide exterior connection for light to be mounted in tree to the west of cabin. Provide all plates and devices. All plate covers to be smooth white Sierra, or equal.

Provide electric baseboard heat throughout. Figure a good quality baseboard and submit pictures and engineering data. Keep heating price separate from rest of bid. The owner will supply all lighting fixtures.

E. Insulation

1. Provide full thick 6" fiberglass batt insulation, all exterior walls.
2. Fill all roof joist spaces with cellulose insulation, or with fiberglass batt insulation.
3. Fill all floor joists with batt insulation.
4. Provide 3" extruded polystyrene (or equal) insulation around interior of entire foundation perimeter walls, down to footings.
5. Provide 6 mill poly vapor barrier on inside of all outside walls and ceiling surfaces.
6. Provide tyveck, all exterior walls.

F. Painting

1. All exterior redwood siding and trim will have one coat primer and two coats exterior paint.
2. All cedar shingles to be unfinished.
3. All redwood soffits to have a natural finish, material to be selected.
4. All windows and sliding doors are wood, metal clad and will have two coats exterior paint.
5. The entry door is metal and will be painted in multi-color pattern, to be determined.
6. Fireplace chimney, one coat primer two coats exterior paint.
7. All interior wood ceilings - one coat transparent stain, wiped, and one coat sealer.
8. All interior pine trim, same as 7.
9. All interior oak walls, 3 coats clear sealer.
10. All interior oak trim, 3 coats sealer.
11. Sheetrock ceiling in #2 bedroom, one coat sealer, one coat paint.
12. All other sheetrock walls to be papered. (Material by owner)
13. Interior surface of all wood windows, 3 coats sealer.

14. All interior surfaces of sliding doors and entry door, 2 coats paint.
15. All interior pine doors to have one coat primer, two coats finish paint.
16. All exterior steel rails to come primed - apply 2 additional coats exterior paint.

G. Flooring
1. All oak flooring shown on plans to be white oak 4" +/- widths, finished with 3 coats polyurethane, non gloss finish.

H. Finish hardware
1. To be selected by owner. Provide $1,200 allowance in estimate.

I. Stove and chimney
1. To be provided by owner, installed by builder. Provide $3,000 allowance in estimate.

J. Kitchen cabinets and all shelving
1. Installed by builder - provide $4,000 allowance.

K. Kitchen appliances
1. To be supplied by owner and installed by contractor.

L. Sauna heater
1. To be supplied by owner, installed by contractor. Provide $550 allowance.

M. Top roof deck (flat)
1. Provide a rubber roof of approved quality. Lay 2x2 treated boards over this, on pitch or mastic, 16" o.c., running east-west to allow drainage. Nail 1x4 redwood deck, spaced 3/8" to these sleepers.

INDEX